The
Voiceless
University

An Argument for
Intellectual Autonomy

Harold Zyskind
Robert Sternfeld

Foreword by Joseph Axelrod

THE
VOICELESS
UNIVERSITY

 Jossey-Bass Inc., Publishers
San Francisco · Washington · London · 1971

THE VOICELESS UNIVERSITY
An Argument for Intellectual Autonomy
      Harold Zyskind and Robert Sternfeld

Copyright © 1971 by Jossey-Bass, Inc., Publishers

Jossey-Bass, Inc., Publishers
San Francisco, California USA

Library of Congress Catalog Card Number 78-132822

International Standard Book Number ISBN 0-87589-103-9

Manufactured in the United States of America
      Composed and printed by York Composition Company, Inc.
      Bound by Chas. H. Bohn & Co., Inc.

JACKET DESIGN BY WILLI BAUM, SAN FRANCISCO

FIRST EDITION

Code 7123

The
Jossey-Bass Series
in Higher Education

General Editors

JOSEPH AXELROD
*San Francisco State College
and University of California, Berkeley*

MERVIN B. FREEDMAN
*San Francisco State College
and Wright Institute, Berkeley*

Foreword

When I first saw an early draft of *The Voiceless University*, I knew that the authors were saying something that was worth listening to; my two rereadings have confirmed that first impression. Indeed, I would say it is a brilliant book.

But the very profundity of *The Voiceless University* will create problems for the reader. For example, the intelligent but too-busy administrator will be frustrated to discover in his hands a book that deserves more time than he has to give. With most books on higher education (or in most fields), he does not face this problem. Some books can be read casually—sampled, as it were—with quite productive results; others cover a variety of standard topics, and their arrangement encourages the busy reader to select only the two or three chapters that are most germane to his work; for research studies, the busy decision maker can limit his efforts to the "Problem" and "Conclusions" chapters, leaving to his subordinates the (often more rewarding) job of sifting through the middle chapters and studying the data.

The Voiceless University, however, is not constructed in a way that allows such reading. All the specific topics that the authors discuss—for example, the use of drugs on the Stony Brook campus, the appropriate roles of faculty members in the classroom, the nature of autonomous ideas—however interesting they may be in themselves, take on their most significant meanings through their relationships to the whole of the authors' argument. The nature of the book thus makes a sampling of selected chapters or a scanning of the whole less productive in this case than usual.

There is a second source of difficulty for the reader of *The*

Foreword

Voiceless University. If he shares the presuppositions commonly held nowadays by writers in higher education, he will expect those assumptions to be held by the present authors as well. But the authors do not accept, for example, the central tenets of the psychosocial approach to the American university taken by most behavioral scientists. Someone who (like myself) shares the presuppositions of the student-development philosophy of education will have quite an adjustment to make. He must persist until he stops wanting to scribble "No" in the margin and begins to listen. Only then can his experience with this book be productive.

Another set of presuppositions that the authors refuse to accept, but which characterize most writings in higher education today, centers around the existence of a power struggle among the several "estates" on campus such as trustees, administrators, faculty members, and students. As we look through the current literature of higher education, we learn from author A or B that one faction or another is winning or losing the power struggle; or from author C that the off-campus establishment has rigged it so that none of the factions can win; or from author D that all sides can win if they follow a certain collaborative model. The readers of *The Voiceless University* who have found such analyses useful (and who are certain the solution is among them somewhere) will be disturbed to discover that the authors find this whole way of thinking about the problems of higher education essentially unproductive.

Since reviewers of books are often strong-minded individuals who insist on reading a book from their point of view and not in terms of its own integral framework, it will be interesting to see how they characterize *The Voiceless University.* I have no doubt that some scholars will place the authors at once in the same "counterrevolutionist" tradition in which W. H. Cowley classifies two of the greatest innovators in American education, Alexander Meiklejohn and Robert Hutchins. Such a characterization, I confess, might be interesting to argue about and play with; but surely the times are too serious to justify spending too many moments on such academic taxonomies.

Moreover, I have no doubt that in today's polarized world

Foreword

of faculty and student conservatives versus faculty and student radicals, some reviewers will want to determine for their readers which "side" this book is on. It will be interesting to see what answer these answer-givers give to this unanswerable question. Faculty and student radicals will feel great antipathy to many of the observations and arguments in *The Voiceless University;* but that is not because the authors are in the conservative camp. And proestablishment faculty and students will find an even larger number of observations and arguments objectionable; but, again, that is not because the authors are in the radical camp. The book is simply too original to fit that—or any other—set of either-or categories.

The Voiceless University is thus not a book that lends itself to easy characterization or categorization—or, indeed, to easy understanding—for it is a new departure in contemporary educational thought. It is not another protest from the prostudent faction, an echo from one of the various faculty camps, another plaint from a pathetic, paralyzed administrator, or another tongue-lashing from a political official purporting to represent the public interest. The book does not speak in the voice of any of these factions. It is the first book, in recent educational literature, to speak for the voiceless university itself.

San Francisco
August 1971

JOSEPH AXELROD
Chairman, Department of
    Comparative Literature
San Francisco State College

Preface

The Voiceless University develops a theory of higher education based on the idea of the university as a center for disciplined thought. So that the idea remains basic throughout, we concentrate on two main tasks—clarifying the nature of the central activity and seeking guidelines from that activity for a better understanding of the responsibilities and rights of the university in the complex roles attributed to it today.

Both these tasks have been slighted in contemporary debate. Most disputants who have studied or taught in the university take it for granted that they know from experience what the central or "academic" activity is, and they deal with the problems of assessing it, redirecting it to useful social goals, and putting it under an egalitarian governance system—or of defending it against such efforts for change. This emphasis, pro or con, is doubly faulty. First, successful experience in academic pursuit does not assure an understanding of its general nature, just as continual use of the memory does not provide a reflective understanding of it. Second, the disputants draw their guidelines from social, economic, or cultural theory rather than from analysis of the particular way in which independent thought bears on social action or of the limits that its autonomy imposes on any governance system.

Further, the activity of thought often appears to be the central object of attention when in fact it is not. When the learning process is studied in terms of psychological principles, it is seen as a change in the student that proceeds by stimulus and response, motivation and satisfaction, and so on. Such analyses are important for psychology, but in a theory of higher education the learning process must be treated instead as a movement of thought—a disciplined development of ideas—whether it takes place in the classroom or in research projects. We treat motivations in *The Voiceless University*, but we do so by focusing on those which are peculiarly appropriate to work and life in the university.

The proper focus in contemporary analyses of the university may be thrown off center also by those who seek to consider the ultimate nature of the knowledge or truth being sought. Such epistemological and metaphysical considerations are important, but in a theory of higher education intended to have practical bearing on the present situation, they can be digressive and restrictive, carrying the implication that only one kind of knowledge should be sought or that the curriculum should be organized by one scheme of the arts and sciences. In *The Voiceless University* we do not seek the metaphysical foundations of disciplined thought but rather take as our starting point the fact that diverse disciplines show us diverse achievements of men engaged in treating isolated subjects and advancing or disseminating knowledge of them by various methods. That is, we seek for the common features of disciplined thought in the form in which men in fact engage in it as they learn and teach. Thus, whereas in comparison with the psychologists' approach we emphasize the intellectual structure of academic pursuits, in comparison with the metaphysical approach we focus on these pursuits as an ongoing process of thought.

In general, then, *The Voiceless University* is addressed to a double need of philosophy of higher education: the theoretical need to focus on its own distinctive subject matter and the practical need to apply the understanding of this subject matter to present problems. Disciplined thought constitutes a distinctive subject matter, we argue, because it has an inherent autonomy; further, an understanding of this autonomy has practical value because it gives a unique character to the various roles of the university as a public service institution, a cultural community, and a new home for the young. Of course, we have yet to explain and prove these claims and make them significant.

Although concerned with the approach to problems rather

than their particular solutions, *The Voiceless University* was generated by and is a response to the issues raised by recurring campus disturbances. Our interest is not in tactics or operational balancing devices for the university in times of crisis but rather in the concepts that crisis discussions have made most prominent. The factual focus from which we selected the issues (besides the common information about universities) was the situation at the State University of New York at Stony Brook, which we have observed in detail. We believe that special features of this institution make it especially suitable for a discussion of the need for voices to speak on behalf of the university today. Accordingly we have drawn a large proportion of our illustrations from events at Stony Brook. They stand on their own as typical cases, but they have more significance if seen in the context of their particular setting. For this purpose, the following background notes should be helpful.

Stony Brook is typical of state university units begun in the northeast section of the country after World War II, when the citizenry finally demanded public higher education (long available in the Midwest, South, and West) that had previously been denied to the Northeast because of the political dominance of alumni from the large, powerful, private universities. The Board of Trustees delayed the establishment of university centers for over ten years, despite the obvious need for them as attested to by commissions and experts in higher education. In this delaying process, they recruited and lost a number of good administrative officers. During this time, they started the institution now at Stony Brook on a temporary campus with a temporary chief administrative officer with a mandate (after the first Sputnik) to prepare college teachers for science. This mandate was interpreted boldly by the first chief administrative officer as requiring ultimately a full-fledged PhD program and he sought faculty for this purpose. A relatively permanent administration was not achieved until the sixth year of the school. Before that, the first student strike in protest of the abrupt transfer of a popular dean of students had successfully (along with other factors) unseated the first president after a tenure of only eight months. During this period, Stony Brook was subjected to pressure from the faculty of a nearby, large, private university to retain their graduates who had not been renewed, as well as pressure from religious groups (including a congressman) to eliminate beatnik poetry readings they found objectionable.

Since the first successful student strike in 1961, Stony Brook has had demonstrations of all kinds, including the more fashionable type in recent years—occupying the library, the infirmary, and the computer center; burning buildings; overturning automobiles—for reasons now standard at most universities, including responses to the widely publicized drug raids by police.

We do not seek here to weigh the results of the demonstrations (although we doubt their net value) because we seek a campus where university business can be done without any demonstrations—disruptive or peaceful—and where the normal channels are responsive to all the proper needs of university personnel. Our concern is with educational principles and how they can be applied to various problems emerging out of the tense situation now pervading our campuses. We suggest ways to recreate the atmosphere of freedom so essential for successful activity on the part of both students and teachers. This freedom demands the absence of solutions imposed from outside the classroom—whether such imposition involves politicians and the police or radicals. We argue here for a basic reorientation that can help restore the conditions of intellectual freedom and integrity without power plays. The dilemma apparent in such a statement—that we need peace as a condition of reorientation and reorientation to restore peace—can be avoided if response to protest is based on prudence and insight. We leave this important question aside in our study, however, for there is an equal urgency in the demand that tentative peace become self-sustaining. This objective depends in turn on the appearance of articulate voices that can suggest what factors should be central to university education and how they can be used to face the problems that plague the times.

Because we have used Stony Brook as a source of many illustrations, it is necessary to note the limitation in our intention. Our concern is not with Stony Brook, as such, but with universities generally, and more particularly with those fairly common features which mark a serious situation on campuses nationally and reveal disturbingly misdirected conceptions of the difficulties. Many events at Stony Brook fell into this pattern. But using them as illustration is not intended to provide a rounded picture of Stony Brook. Had that been our purpose we should have had to describe many unmentioned features, including the known excellences of some of its students, faculty, and administration.

The Voiceless University is organized to allow a recurrent interplay between our general approach and its application to the problems that occasioned it. The first chapter describes the prevailing view of the university crisis in the late sixties to show how the debate was thrown off its proper center. Of the five main parts of the book, two (Parts One and Three) are weighted on the theoretical side, the first part developing the general principles of the university as built around disciplined thought and the third part making an internal analysis of the nature of that thought. The practical parts (Two and Four) treat problems of curriculum, drugs, teaching methods, and so on. The fifth part draws the argument together by looking at the university as (in Whitehead's phrase) an "enduring object" in a context of change.

In the preparation of *The Voiceless University* we benefited from the reactions and suggestions of students and faculty colleagues in informal and formal discussions at the State University of New York at Stony Brook (SUSB). We cannot here list the persons and occasions, but we want to single out the continued interest and conversations of Theodore Bronsnick, a former student, and the discussion at Cardozo College that followed our presentation of some of the main ideas in the book.

We are also grateful for the suggestions, criticisms, and expertise of colleagues on the problems of specific chapters: Joseph Axelrod, San Francisco State College (Chapter Eleven); Elizabeth Coleman, New School for Social Research (Two, Nine, Eleven); Maurice Cramer, Pennsylvania State University (Nine); Leonard Eisenbud, SUSB (Eight); Erich Goode, SUSB (Seven); Norman Goodman, SUSB (Six); Patrick Hill, SUSB (One, Five); William

Preface

Lister, SUSB (Eight); Velio Marsocci, SUSB (Six); Abram V. Martin, Grand Valley State College (Eight); Merrill Rodin, New School for Social Research (Nine, Eleven); Thomas Rogers, SUSB (Nine); Walter Watson, SUSB (Two, Four, Five); Charles Wegener, University of Chicago, for joint staff work in the past (Nine); and Humanities staffs of the College, University of Chicago, for discussions in the past of various works and topics considered in Ten and Eleven. Thanks are due also to the Graduate School, SUSB, for a grant for secretarial assistance and for the skillful assistance of Terri Davidson, Nancy Hoffman, and Susan Knorr.

Stony Brook, New York   HAROLD ZYSKIND
August 1971   ROBERT STERNFELD

Contents

Contents

The Voiceless University

An Argument for
Intellectual Autonomy

Circumstances
of
Crisis

 1

The guiding principle of this book is that the mission of the university should be drawn from internal factors—that is, from the nature of ideas as determined through processes of inquiry and communication. This statement becomes controversial in the context of this decade because it means that the structure and purpose of the university are not drawn directly from the nature of youth or from general social conditions or from the immediate needs of the times. Rather the inherent potential of the internal factors makes these other factors relevant to the university.

At their core, these significant internal factors have been the same from the Greek Academy and Lyceum to the contemporary multiversity. We think Cardinal Newman was right to seek *the* idea of a university, for this idea should be what differentiates the institutions and processes of higher education from others in society, as well as what provides a stable base of internal continuity. Such a suggestion is likely to be met with resistance today, however, on the ground that the pace of change and the disappearance of the ivory tower preclude any fixed idea. Our counterargument is that in this kind of complex, fluid context, thought about higher

The Voiceless University

education goes more easily adrift, creating a need for a sense of a stable center—of the idea of a university.

But even with the assumption of a constant idea, it is important to restate and reexplore that idea with every major shift of circumstance. Otherwise, it rigidifies, as in the minds of those who once came to identify it with knowledge of Greek and Latin. Or it dissipates, as we think it has today. An adequate idea of the university must be able to serve as a starting point for coping with the peculiar difficulties and opportunities that confront the university today. Thus, although our purpose is to reexplore *the* idea of the university, we need to begin with its circumstantial setting, which for the purpose of this discussion can be considered the primary period of the campus revolt—1964–1969. It is interesting that this revolt has come hard upon the efforts of university leaders to reconceive (or de-conceive) the multiversity as being most things to most men; such vagueness of conception makes the university a "perfect" target for the rising—and amorphous—discontents of the young. The revolt of 1964–1969 was also amorphous, but for that reason it tended to bring into view the full diversity of forces at work. We begin therefore with this revolt as a pulse-taking measure for our special purpose rather than as historical coverage. The point for us is that the problems and challenges raised by the revolt were not resolved—or dissolved—and therefore constitute the background against which to test any discussion of the idea of the university.

EXTERNAL THREAT

The external relations of the university had considerable effect on the internal situation during the revolt. The radicals hoped to make their internal revolt a part or moment of their attack on the social structure in general. The society reacted repressively, and the repressive measures were met in turn by resistance from a large part of the university community. At times the conflict appeared to resemble that of the fifties, when the antagonists were clearly the universities on the one side and political agencies and much of the public press on the other. In our period, too, state legislatures and

Congress have threatened and have in fact passed punitive legisla-tion.[1] Various investigative bodies have sought the signs and causes of campus trouble. At Stony Brook, for example, the president and other officials were called to testify at public hearings; the county grand jury issued lengthy reports calling for the dismissal of certain officials; the local police conducted undercover activities in the search—so common talk had it—for Communist influence no less than for drug-law violators; and a massive midnight raid on the eve of exams to gather up alleged drug violators brought loud public praise of the police officer in charge. This situation resembled the antiuniversity attacks of the postwar period in intensity of feeling and in the type of investigative exposés, which reveal that the public viewed the university in the same educative terms as it does a regimented grade school. The integrity of the university was at stake in both periods.

But the difference between the periods is critical. In the fifties, the overt issue was relatively clear, the focus being the politi-cal or ideological credentials for teaching. And the university com-munity was united both in its view that the real issue was academic freedom and in its commitment to self-defense and counterattack. But in the sixties, the overt issues were many—drugs, disruption, ROTC, black studies, governance, depersonalization, among others. There still is little agreement (although no less sloganeering) on what the real issue is; in fact, if anything there has been active dis-unity.

Although McCarthyism in the fifties was damaging enough, it could not penetrate far (except in unconscionable injury to some individuals) or establish control of the university when countered by the comparative unity in action and conception of the problem by the university community. The sixties, on the other hand, leave us with perilous vacuums. To many, the trouble is not that administra-tors are doing the wrong things but that they are doing little or nothing. To compound the problem, if it is desirable to take a costly

[1] M. O. Hatfield, "Public Pressures on Higher Education," in G. K. Smith (Ed.), *The Troubled Campus: Current Issues in Higher Education 1970* (San Francisco: Jossey-Bass, 1970), lists and explains such legislation.

The Voiceless University

stand against outside forces in defense of principle, there are only vague or incompatible notions of what that principle is.

An ironic fact is that one such principle offered as a baseline for a university stand could easily justify the entry of the public directly into university affairs. This principle, the new rule of governance, suggests that every individual should have voice and vote in any decisions affecting his life. Taken simplistically (as it often is in discussions of university governance), the rule runs up against the obvious fact that the taxpayer is vitally affected by decisions made in the university on such issues as curricula and standards. A faithful application of the rule would therefore give the taxpaying public at large a voice and vote in university governance. Such taxpayers have provoked the impulse to repressive legislation, which is aggravated by the fact that the pace of thrust and counterthrust can accelerate so fast—on one side, from petition to demands and from insults to building seizures; on the other, from permissiveness to momentary states of martial law.

As the pace intensified, many deliberative defenders of the university—outside as well as within—seemed to anticipate Richard Nixon in their view of where the remedy lay. They were convinced that the difficulty lies in minority rule by radicals because of the inactivity of the moderates. Believing that the majority of students and faculty belonged to the center, they thought that it was necessary to energize the inertial group in the center—the "silent majority." We opposed this view of the university population before Nixon expanded it to include the whole population, and we believe that many university officials are still caught up in the illusions and snares of this view. Let us look, then, at the student revolt in terms of this issue.

ILLUSORY SILENT CENTER

Police brutality at Columbia and at other campuses (such as Berkeley) energized the silent center into following the radicals. Many have interpreted this radicalization to mean that, while the center was moderate on the substantive issues, it felt that all had to respond to the radicals' plea for resistance to police power abuses.

4

But this interpretation is open to question, as a number of disruptions at Stony Brook suggest. We take, for example, the outbreaks and subsequent strikes of the spring of 1969. Late one evening, the police came in some force—several cars—purportedly to arrest some students on previously determined charges of drug-law violations. It was the eve of exams. News of the raid spread throughout the campus. Without direction, without leadership, students poured out of the dormitories in a rage and moved across the campus. A gate house was burned, and considerable other damage was done. Although we were not eyewitnesses of these events, no one denies that there was a spontaneous surge of violence. Nor is there doubt on the point on which we wish to focus: the radical leadership was not the main cause of this outburst.

How is this spontaneous rage to be explained then? Of course, one can note that in this case the repressive intent of the police proved the radicals' argument. But to that statement must be added the fact confirmed by the Stony Brook outburst—namely, that an overwhelming majority of the student body was ready to be aroused. There was of course some cooling, but the students' rage was easily renewed by fiery leaders. (A staggering number of them in open meeting authorized a full-page ad in the *New York Times* marked by its excited non sequiturs.[2] And this in turn was

[2] The full text of the ad for which the students paid several thousand dollars of their own money was: "We the student body of S.U.N.Y. at Stony Brook wish to make it clear that Monday night's drug arrests were politically motivated. It is no mere coincidence that the raid occurred the night before the Hughes Committee was to reconvene for hearings on University drug policy. It is quite obvious that the raid was intended specifically to discredit the University and its administrators before the Committee and to create an atmosphere which would condone tighter restrictions and increase infiltration of our campus. While we would agree to charges of gross incompetence in certain members of our administration, the tactics used to demonstrate this are nothing less than Machiavellian. Those who engineered the raid obviously did not have our welfare in mind and were more interested in furthering their own political careers by witch hunting on our campus, than in restricting drug traffic at Stony Brook. This can do nothing to alleviate our problems, it can only exacerbate the situation. Because the atmosphere of repression that has been created here will hinder serious and honest intellectual pursuits, we are attempting to suspend all normal functions for the remainder of the

5

followed by a strike of normal classes.) The development of events at Stony Brook suggested—as did the crises at Cornell, Harvard, and other campuses—that the center was not in the center at all; for all practical purposes, it was the silent left.

Thus, when the great majority of silent students spoke up, they spoke up for the left—specifically for a left whose first impulse is to strike back against the administration or external forces by paralyzing the university. Such an impulse is inappropriately separate from the idea of the university, for it neither defends the university from outside forces nor seeks to restore its internal balance.

The explanation of the students' behavior must lie elsewhere. Why was the moderate, silent mass so easily moved to the left? To ask this question is to realize that they were not so silent. They spoke—still speak—forcibly of the generation gap: their parents do not understand them any more than the university officials. On each of the sociopolitical issues of the times—Vietnam, racism, poverty, pollution, suburbia—they express intense criticism of, and alienation from, the Establishment. Their response to the university appears to be an extension of this general alienation. They were silent in that they did not publicize their views as did the aggressive radicals, but they did not conceal them in face-to-face relations or in campus affairs. As individuals they were forceful in charging that the administration was deceitful and timid, the teaching bad, the curriculum irrelevant, and all procedures depersonalized. They allowed for exceptions but basically said what the radicals said. Thus, what students said on such issues was not very complicated, and it was more or less uniform.

---

term through a non-violent strike of classes. The University must recognize the necessity for a governance structure that is responsive to the needs of the entire University Committee. We can no longer tolerate the duplicity and constant acquiescence of our campus administrators to the political realities of local and state agencies. We will no longer tolerate the absence of effective administrative leadership which has created an environment encouraging violence from within and abuse from without. We strongly condemn the rape of our University and the sacrifice of our fellow students by politicians who mask their ambition in law and order campaigns, and we refuse to lend our support to the lie that education is possible in a state of repression" ("The Rape of Stony Brook," *New York Times*, May 16, 1969, p. 53).

Circumstances of Crisis

Although there are differences between moderates and radicals in the desired scope and tempo of change, they are still in fundamental agreement that manifold ills beset us, and the discontents gnaw away. These common discontents keep the moderates sympathetic with the radicals in times of relative calm and minimize the differences in a crisis. The moderates were susceptible to the emotion-charged provocation at Stony Brook, not because the claim of repression seemed proved by the raid, but more likely because the radicals' claim that the students are totally repressed suddenly seemed to be the explanation, to most students, of all their discontents. By that act of instant synthesis, the center became radical. And since the radical view sees almost anything as a symptom of something fundamental, a strike at anything—a car, a window, a classroom—is an emotional strike at the system in general more than at an institution in particular.

ESCALATION

Such a sense of the situation probably lies behind one kind of response made by many administrators and faculty; namely, they presented themselves as ready to correct some of the ills that exist within the university or to initiate steps for a fundamental restructuring of it. The hypothesis was that the university would end disruptions by redressing the grievances that provoked them. The bolder administrators at the same time reminded the nation that until the injustices outside the university were remedied, the situation in the universities would remain on the brink.

However, this kind of response allowed the disrupters to conclude that the university authorities accepted the validity of the students' complaints yet would have done nothing without the disruption. This view of the indispensability of disruption to reform of the universities became common, having the understanding of such men as Tom Wicker of the *New York Times*. The Establishment responded only to pressure, but under pressure it confessed and conceded something. When it stiffened and criticized students, the criticism tended to be directed only to student methods or manners—not to the substance of their grievances.

The Voiceless University

The university authorities seemed to have no alternative response to this supposed indispensability of disruption. None of their actions seemed capable of providing anything more than temporary quiet. The ills were what made the students ripe for radicalism, the reasoning went, and so long as these sources of discontent existed there would be more disruptions.

According to this hypothesis, then, major reforms should have had a calming effect. But the experience at Stony Brook proved otherwise, even when the reforms were responsive to major grievances. Apart from external matters, such as the Vietnam war, students were intensely concerned with two goals: a closer link between living and learning, and freedom of choice in subjects of study. The first challenge was met fairly early by substantial efforts of the administration to transform dormitories into colleges with self-determined intellectual and artistic projects involving faculty; the students of an experimental college planned their curriculum on the go and wholly merged living and studying. On the second issue of student participation in shaping curriculum, the action was more dramatic. The pressure for curtailment of fixed-distribution requirements and for independent-study programs was intense. About three thousand students petitioned the faculty for immediate passage of a curriculum committee plan that leaned toward laissez faire and was itself a response to the pressure. The speeches of student leaders, made at a faculty meeting, virtually turned the petition into a menacing demand. The plan, which normally would have taken far longer to formulate and approve, was instituted immediately. We do not say here that the faculty was not acting from conviction but only that the action did formally give the students much of what they had been demanding in fact and all of it in principle.

But it was very shortly after this major change that the midnight rampage and subsequent strike occurred. The curriculum reform had not assuaged the general discontent but instead seemed to have lowered the psychological boiling point on campus. Success seemed to have whetted the appetite of the students. They demanded in the strike after the drug raid that exams be delayed or discounted; and in fact all students were permitted to take a pass/fail in all courses if they wished. Thereafter, other conditions that had been regarded as minor or even necessary frustrations were cited more and more by more and more students as proof of the existence of an all-embracing intolerable system of repression. The silent left had gone momentarily radical.

Was the real reason behind the union of the supposed center and the radicals the fact that the radical cause was justified? We do not wish to dispute the radicals' position on the social issues, since we discuss it in later chapters (Three, Four, Six). But their views of change within the university invite considerable doubt about their assessment of the ills or the remedies—especially about the importance they ascribe to such matters as the pass/fail grade option. Further, not only was the curriculum reform itself debatable in principle as well as in fact, but the tendency to escalate irritations into revolution should often have been enough to make the grievance suspect.

Where then were the counterarguments? Where was the other voice of the university? It seemed that the dominant tendency among the older generation within the university—who wished to separate themselves from the law-and-order slogans of the unappreciative public—was to say, in effect, "yes, there are many things wrong; the university is in bad shape. We only plead that the reform be at a reasonable pace." This response seemed to assume that whatever is not yet changed is in need of it. Thus, the university establishment actually showed itself to be another variant of the radical view—a paler version in its aversion to wholesale leaps but nonetheless similar in the direction of change assumed. This similar bent was even true of such "tough" administrations as S. I. Hayakawa's at San Francisco State. The radicals provided most of the substantive arguments on the nature of the university today. The best that the university authorities did on the whole—besides agreeing on how great is the need for change—was to argue that violence does not belong in a university. They were largely silent about what *does* belong in it.

Here then, right or wrong, was a key reason for the preva-

The Voiceless University

lence of the radical views: there was and is a dearth of counter-arguments on the substantive issues. It is the silence of the faculty, more than of the administration, that creates the most notable vacuum. Words are said, but the voice is the echo, in various watered-down forms, of the voices of the radicals.

THE ISSUE

With even moderate students focused on their radical discontents and with authorities following a policy of confession and concession, most reflective thought and dialogue has tended toward autopsylike discussions. Criticism can be life-restoring perhaps. What we find notable about the present effort is that failure of the university is discussed in terms of how it has failed to cope with psychological and sociopolitical factors, rather than how it has fallen short of its mission to disseminate and advance knowledge. The psychological approach today makes basic such problems as identity, life styles, and personal relations in a depersonalizing context, especially as these affect youth. It is then assumed that the idea of the university is to contribute to the resolution of these life problems. The call is generated for living/learning situations, for programs centered on the development of creativity and self-expression, and for egalitarian devices that even consider such minutiae as whether all members of a learning group should be on a first-name basis. The sociopolitical approach—not necessarily incompatible with the first—takes the university as a microcosm of the society and sees educational problems as problems of practical relevance and innovation—in general, problems of revolution and tradition.

These approaches can seriously alter the original function of the university as a center for disciplined inquiry. The role assigned to the classroom provides a prime example. Both the psychological and sociopolitical perspectives[3] agree in deemphasizing the classroom, or at least in opposing the conception of it as a center for the intellectual development of a subject matter as taught by its master.

[3] We do not purport to cover the diverse theories developed in these disciplines (such as that of Edward Shils) but, as indicated, only those that have justified or articulated the ferment and revolt.

10

To the new approaches, such a classroom process is neither personalized nor actional and so must be renovated or eliminated.

Our concern in this book is to test such claims. We have no quarrel with the call for self-development, social action, and other psychological and social values. Rather we question whether one should take these goals as the proper starting point for educational theory, especially for a theory designed to determine the activities to which the university should devote itself. We hold that the starting point should instead be the activities inherent in the nature of a university—such as disciplined thought—that are developed in a classroom. From a better understanding of these activities, one can then determine which contributions can be made to critical psychological and social problems. The issue, then, is not whether the university should help deal with these problems, but how—in a way set by extrinsic considerations or in the way set by the special business of a university.

The option sounds deceptively formal: whether to go in thought from psychosocial factors to the classroom or from the classroom to psychosocial factors. However, the difference can be crucial, as we shall see. Let us first examine the classroom aspect of the issue and then fan out to the broader problems.

Principles

❧ ONE ❧

Part One states the principles bound up with universities as they are found in the key university activity (Chapter Two), in its organization (Chapter Three), and in its inherent ends (Chapter Four). These chapters thus constitute the foundations upon which the rest of the book is built. Yet the building of the rest of the book is by no means a simple deductive process, as we shall indicate in the introductions to the subsequent parts.

The statement of principles in Chapter One centers on the key university activity and argues the autonomy of the university as the locus of this special activity. The university's organization and operation is then shown to be, in large measure, determined by this autonomous activity. And finally, successful university activity is identified with the ends of student idealists—some of whom have felt that ordinary university activity must be disrupted in order for them to pursue their ideals.

Centrality
of the
Classroom

 2

The classroom has proved a frequent and ready target of attack whenever campus ferment reaches crisis level. Militants have denied entry to selected classes, have interrupted classes in progress, or have called strikes against all classes. Often the administration and faculty have joined the trend: at Stony Brook, for example, classes were canceled for three days in order to provide time for discussion of university problems. During two other spring crises, classes were allowed to meet to discuss the grievances behind a strike.

Although such responses may have been excessive, they reflect a general decline in the status of the classroom that is evident in the normal workings of the university as well. Student leaders express increasing hostility to the traditional roles of authoritarian expert and passive student and welcome experimental plan-as-you-go group learning. Faculty attitudes also contribute to the breakdown: professors may lightly cancel classes for professional activities or personal convenience. The system of rewards is such that a professor's goal is to replace teaching time with research time. The motive of engaging undergraduates in a discipline and of testing the effort partly by their responses to it still operates but with very limited status.

14

Centrality of the Classroom

There are many attitudes shared by faculty and student that also undercut the value of the classroom. The professors who seem to care most for the students as individuals, run their classes in a free-wheeling, open-ended way—that is, in a "nonclassroom" way—or else they invest much effort outside of class in socializing and advising. Because such professors are so popular and the student/ faculty interactions they create so strongly supported today, it is worthwhile to examine the arguments behind their popularity. We will give some coherence to these arguments for the obsolescence of the classroom by discussing four aspects: the student, the subject matter appropriate to him, the abilities to be developed in him, and the available instructional materials.

Today's student comes into the university with a very large part of his knowledge attributable to sources other than the classroom, such as television and the teenage subcultures, in which the senses are dynamically brought into play and the emotions are inextricably involved with acts of learning. Proponents of this argument maintain that today's student accordingly requires educational processes that engage the whole person. They see today's university teaching as thin and static, providing a purely auditory experience drained of the necessary emotional involvement.

This argument extends to subject matter, maintaining that the university classroom deals in abstractions and dead data, rather than the stimulating, concrete subject matter necessary to take hold of a mind. The alternative subject matter should also be geared to the "now" emphasis of today's youth, and, above all, subjects and ideas must be relevant to action and not pure intellectualization.

The array of technical data supplied by today's education requires robotlike assimilation and furthermore is soon obsolete. Methods are needed more than matter, they argue, and the matter should not consist of tired repetitions (that present classroom procedure encourages) but fresh views. Similarly, the methods themselves should not be routine, but innovative.

It follows that the focus of education should be self-expression (to encourage the discovery of identity) and creativity. There are no routine rules for discovering one's identity and achieving the dignity and self-dependence that go along with it, for such discovery depends on intuitive insight, a sudden flash, or a release of inner springs. So it is not surprising that this argument sees contemporary classroom instruction as abounding in rules set forth routinely or mechanically, and therefore antipathetic to processes of discovery.

The key to freshness of thought and feeling, according to this argument, is found in the new relationship of man to the communication media. The media bombard us with a multiplicity of facts and sense stimuli simultaneously; the problem for youth is not simply to take in what is transmitted but to *synthesize* it and pattern it into a comprehensible whole. Because the patterning must be his own doing, it can be the central feature of the creative process. Thus, the conventional classroom must give way to imaginative new ways of employing technological media. In addition to these new materials, a need is seen for replacing the formal procedures of the conventional classroom with unplanned interaction among people; free play in such interaction should allow each individual to participate in his own way and so advance the common enterprise.

Such arguments for innovation and individual expression dominate the popular forums today. However, we feel the rhetorical package in which they are wrapped further subverts the status of the classroom in that the proponents often present themselves as nonacademic (in the way that men seeking public office like to say they are not politicians) and frequently, as antiprofessional. In the present circumstances the sweeping character of this iconoclasm has an effective appeal which carries over to the attack on the classroom. But apart from such rhetoric their position is justifiably opposed to the classroom as they conceive it. But how well does their conception fit the facts? Undoubtedly, it does apply to very many classroom courses. But to leap from these cases to a view of classroom courses as naturally or inherently lockstep routines is unwarranted. We believe that the proponents of this view have lost sight of what some classes are and what far more of them can and ought to be. As a basis for our position we define "classroom activity" as the teacher-student contacts in which the center of discourse is a finite object of inquiry grounded in a broader context, with each contact or session being a step toward the overall development of ideas *inherent* in the given subject matter.[1] This definition is itself read by some persons to mean that the classroom is the place where lockstep instruction or mechanical transmission of material occurs. To interpret it thus is to view any systematically guided and disciplined inquiry through anticlassroom lenses. Even the defenders of the classroom put on those lenses when they say: "But memorization (or drill) is necessary." A reconception of the meaning of disciplined teaching and learning at a university level is needed; we will devote the remainder of this chapter to our reconception.

We argue that what is central to such a reformation and what provides the strongest basis for its extension into other areas of personality and community is its dependence on *autonomous ideas*. Later in this chapter we deal directly with the structure and workings of such ideas, but we begin with the teacher and student in whom autonomous ideas can work.

TEACHER

Some discontented students desire that the professor be more than a simple researcher or teacher. They want him to be a wise man who is admirable and impressive in all phases of his life and personality. Obviously, the modern professor, for the most part, does not qualify as the Socrates or guru figure desired by the students. He is the kind of man who can have impressive command of a body of significant knowledge while mismanaging his private and civic life. The student is sensitive to the fact that a professor's expertise does not carry any guarantees of the kind of life or posture toward life that goes with it. Many students have become alienated from most adults and from the adult-made world and therefore find it difficult to sit at the feet of a man who appears before them simply as project-bound researcher or topic-bound teacher. They seek a

[1] See also our redefinition on page 25.

17

model of wisdom whose wisdom orders his character and life around peace and morality.

We believe that the search for such men is impractical and mistaken. The classroom of Socrates, as described in the Platonic dialogues, is indeed a model. But in the large it obviously is unrealistic. We are seeking for a system that can be effective for millions of students and hundreds of thousands of instructors and professors. The wise men among adults and the geniuses among the young are too few for our concern. In passing them by, however, we are not settling for an inferior goal. We seek in the classroom what is most *teachable*. The young seeking a guru neglect just this question of *teachability*. We doubt whether wisdom can be taught directly. Even Socrates disclaimed responsibility for the way his disciples turned out. He denied that he was a teacher at all; and noted that the reputedly great men could not impart their own virtues even to their sons. Living in the presence of a great man should be an enriching experience; but nonetheless his whole way of life is too complex, individual, and indivisible for direct transmission.

Because wisdom in itself cannot be taught discursively (if at all), students tend to devalue discursive methods of teaching and to judge great teaching in terms of the teacher's personality, style, humanity, and inspiration. But this too often results in a debasing of wisdom itself, as when we were told by a young woman that the proof that Professor X was the greatest teacher in her experience was that she remembered him vividly, even though she could not remember the subject he taught. Youth should begin asking anew an old question: what *is* teachable, what makes it so, and what is its value? These questions are examined in chapters Eight to Eleven, but we can indicate here our general point, again finding Socrates to be an instructive example. Perhaps because wisdom cannot be implanted or evoked directly, he did not seek simply to open up horizonless vistas of truth. The direct exchanges he had were discursive, focusing on a restrictedly finite structure of discourse. The key to his teaching was this sharp zeroing in—the power to develop a single idea, some "simple little question," in a perspicuous, disciplined, and persuasive way. We take that fact to be a model feature for today's classroom, and we believe that Socrates' method can respond to youth's search for the model of the wise man; for although wisdom cannot be transmitted directly, nonetheless the stimulation provided by disciplined inquiry provides as good a chance as there is for awakening wisdom indirectly.

What sort of person, then, should the teacher be for a viable classroom situation? To call him a researcher who transmits his knowledge is misleading. If he does research and teaches in mathematics, he should be a mathematician; if in chemistry, a chemist, and so on. To characterize him by such labels goes beyond naming a job he performs or a skill he has; saying someone is a mathematician lies between naming his specialty and characterizing his total personality. On the surface, a term like *mathematician* does not seem nearly so encompassing as *wise man* or *fool,* because these terms imply something about the man's civic responsibility, family life, and values that *mathematician* does not. However, being a mathematician does involve attitudes, feelings, and habits bound up with pursuing and doing mathematics. Rarely is he only a mechanical rule follower. He discovers problems, responds to difficulties, seeks to generate a flash of insight, celebrates outcomes—all are operations also found in inquiry and discourse in nearly any field. There are features special to each. A mathematician engages in the magical act of manipulating invisible objects, the diagrams he draws being but symbols of immaterial concepts or entities. Further, he elaborates the logic of their relations. Similarly, other disciplines can and should engage one in actualizing a distinctive power of man. Accordingly, a classroom can be any place—a room or the agora—where a mathematical demonstration, chemical experiment, or literary critique can be so developed that its inseparable by-product becomes an exhibition of what it means, emotionally as well as intellectually, to be a mathematician, chemist, or critic and to interact with other persons as such.

The teacher's act is not like events in plays or stories that motivate a youth to want to become, say, a doctor because of the aura of the white coat and stethoscope and the grateful tears of the heroine. The fine points of this difference define the uniqueness of the university classroom. Disciplines can be presented in several ways; the manner can be *rhetorical,* as when the benefits and fun of being a chemist are described; or *psychological,* as when the subject matter is adapted to the limitations and simple abilities of a young child; or finally, *disciplinary,* as when what is done in, say, chemistry, is done as a chemist would do it. This third feature of discipline marks the university level and specifically the classroom within it. A classroom becomes a place in which such an event constitutes a communication between teacher and learner.[2]

In sum, when the classroom functions as it should and can, then chemist, chemistry, and teacher merge into one; to teach is to do chemistry; and to do chemistry is to be a chemist. Of course, chemists differ from each other, but, equally important, there are different modes of discourse available to them. Some courses or presentations are systematically deductive, and others should be problematic inquiries that generate an innovation or discovery. Being a chemist is being a person who can present proofs as well as discover truths; it is natural that there be courses or phases of courses concerned with problems dependent on both kinds of ability.

A single session, however, is not enough in itself to qualify as a genuine classroom event; it must be seen as part of the development of a larger inquiry. The sense of this larger context and the progression of steps in the inquiry as they emerge from the back of the chemist's mind and go toward what is beyond is also needed to grasp who the teacher is. There is nothing esoteric about this contact of student with instructor. When the student grasps why it is appropriate or necessary that the next step in the course comes when it does, he is figuratively inside the chemist's mind.

Our view should not be seen as separating the chemist from his being as a person. Although he has other kinds of experience, doing chemistry in interaction with students is as complete an en-

---

[2] The categories set up here are chosen to highlight the distinctiveness of the disciplinary method. As we indicate later, we believe that it is itself flexibly adaptable to the rhetorical and psychological factors prominent at lower levels.

gagement of himself as any other. When Archimedes ran unclothed through the streets shouting "Eureka!" he was merely reciting an abstract equation to himself. Similarly, the professor as professional may not think of his family or civic life but that does not prove whether he is engaged in his discipline as a whole man.

Professional activity, taken as an emotional/intellectual experience in the fullest sense, can be looked at as an end in itself— indeed as one of the noblest activities of man. We do not say that the activity is more important than trying to raise the income of the underprivileged by picketing on their behalf. But we do say that providing food to the underprivileged is given more significance when seen as making it less difficult for them to join or rejoin others in such distinctively human experiences as those actualized in the university classroom.

While students on the one hand seek the wise man, they also sometimes complain of the authoritarian role of the professor. His status, they say, eliminates equality and inhibits the free development and expression by each individual of his own views on the subject. The sort of teacher needed, according to this argument, is one who is skillful at drawing people out but who does not insist that his own views predominate as everybody is entitled to his own opinion. We find the proposal of dubious value. Free exchanges of views are desirable, but they fail to fulfill the function of a university classroom and are not central to the educational process (except in advanced graduate or postdoctoral seminars where everyone shares a grounding in the criteria by which to judge the value of what is said).

But our position is not incompatible with student objections to authoritarianism. We said that in the classroom three things merged into a single person—chemistry, chemist, and teacher. Accordingly the students must be at an intellectual level adequate for them to follow an expert explaining and defending himself. The relationship between expert and follower in this case does not fit conventional conceptions of the relationship. The professor is not an authority giving his conclusions, as a medical doctor gives to his patient, nor should he be the great man preaching inspirationally

21

from the mountaintop, nor a one-way transmitter of information. Since the communication must be in terms of the discipline itself, he is rather the expert trying to make his reasoning cogent to others; he is bound to depend on the feedback from them—including the judgments they give on what he says and does. The function of these judgments is not to indicate whether the students personally like his arguments, but rather to point out to the teacher-expert whether his arguments are intelligible and cogent (as distinct from authoritarian, rhetorical, or mechanical). The student has both the opportunity and the responsibility to judge the arguments—he renders a kind of verdict.

Here we have on both sides the motives for a rational interchange and the bases of mutual respect in the classroom. The source of the student's power to make judgment will be discussed later; the point here is that the teacher in a university is somewhat of a dependent expert and the student an autonomous follower. So conceived, each obviously needs the other, yet functions as his own man in the classroom interaction. This double relationship is one of the most satisfying possible, or even conceivable, among men.

STUDENT

Let us inquire then about this student whose views can have such weight. The apparent danger in the study of a discipline on its own terms is that one may thereby be forcing the student's mind from its natural bent. Rousseau, for example, planned Émile's education to actualize nature's intention in him. For Plato, learning was coming to know one's self. And modern psychologists point out the advantages of letting the young college student dwell on vague generalizations because such mental play is good for one of his age. These approaches are all student oriented in that their focus is on learning as a means of enabling the mind to develop its own powers. This approach, in its contemporary form, focuses on subjectivity.

Francis Bacon, on the other hand, gave compelling arguments against the mind's following its own dispositions. However effective those mental bents might be in constructing fantasies or building neat but irrelevant systems, Bacon saw them as tending to

22

foreclose the roads to innovation and discovery in the fields of knowledge. For centuries knowledge had been relatively static, and learning had suffered because men fell into the ills that the mind is heir to—regulating their inquiries by what Bacon called "idols" of overgeneralization and oversimplification. Left on their own, our minds by no means aim straight at the truth of things. We leap to conclusions, substitute words for things, theories for facts, imagination for reason. Bacon felt his contribution to be a set of rules and methods by which the mind could come upon new truths of the world outside it rather than dwell on internal, self-contained constructs. From Aristotle to Russell, it has been pointed out how far from the truth are our minds' first perceptions of the way things are. Thus, Bacon would view education as a process of moving away from the mind's unaided tendencies and opinions toward knowledge generated by methods adapted to the nature of things—methods today called objective.

This opposition between subjectivists and objectivists appears to be of practical importance, although it certainly has produced a recurrent simplification of problems of educational theory to the question of whether subjects should be shaped to students' minds or students' minds to subject disciplines. This has, in turn, produced recurrent cycles in actual curricular programs. The "cafeteria" system of electives provoked reaction in the form of required general education programs, which, in turn, have provoked counterreaction in the form of the current plan-as-you-go independent study orientation. (The double cycle will be completed with the inevitable next swing back to some plan for bringing order into the emergent anarchy.)

But while a certain amount of fanfare heralds all such changes, curriculum development and change proceed to a large extent independently of the simplified mind/matter opposition. The classroom—the immense battery of courses—provides the means for the development and diffusion of these changes in the sphere of ongoing thought. The classroom system is not inherently opposed to innovation; the educational process is a "system" only in the sense that it is set up to keep curricula abreast of advances in the

23

disciplines and to keep the work of the disciplines open to feedback from classroom experience. The continual process of dropping and adding courses makes the system a naturally experimental enterprise. But admittedly the requirement that new ideas be run through the processes of the classroom system also serves a screening function. There are intellectual standards of disciplined analysis appropriate to the classroom but not requisite for some of the peripheral activities to which some like to turn. The application of these standards encourages the kind of new ventures that are likely to have the far-reaching relevance that characterizes disciplined work.

Although we maintain that the concept of mind/matter opposition is less important than the classroom system for a theory of higher education, there remains the question of whether the procedures of the disciplines themselves can be thought of as having a mind orientation or a matter orientation, in the inclusive sense we have given these terms here. We oppose the anticlassroom argument which holds that all disciplines are matter oriented because they are split up into departmentalized professions. We also find misleading the common view that they tend to be polarized— that is, that at one extreme the arts are soft, and at the other the sciences are hard. We prefer to judge by what the disciplines do and are set up to do. From this standpoint, it seems clear that while they vary greatly in their emphases, all of them have significant features of both orientations. For example, art appreciation— even in its more subjective forms—depends on a grasp of the operational necessities under which the artist produced his work, and the work itself is subject to the logic of criticism. These features— necessities and logic—although peculiar to art, still constitute objective dimensions. Conversely, science has a range that extends to the subjective, for it is a truism that the scientist operates to a great extent by art. An extreme example of this range in science is indicated in T. S. Kuhn's *The Structure of Scientific Revolutions*. He shows the radical difference between the objective method used to elaborate consequences of a given scientific theory and the method used to settle claims of competing theories, which depends on preferential feelings and faith.

24

Centrality of the Classroom

The fact that the subjective-objective range is fundamental to a discipline means that to explore a subject or problem within the discipline involves shifts in emphasis between mind and matter orientation. For example, the inquiry will require some moments or phases that are imaginative and some that must be rule-bound, some speculative and others empirical, some synthesizing and others classificatory, some intuitive and others mediated, and so on. This versatility should be reflected accordingly in classroom activity—such activity being redefined here as an expert's opening up of a disciplined structure of thought to the understanding and free judgment of learners prepared to make the judgment. So conceived, this activity can remain inclusive and diversified and can avoid a mind/matter opposition.

One reason that some teaching today is below what it should be is not that it is too discipline-bound but rather that some faculty are not sensitive enough to the potential versatility within the discipline. No doubt nearly all faculty are aware of the diversity, but a regrettable number do not make their courses reflect it.

If we will restore the classroom to its place at the center of the educational process—reducing mechanically uniform teaching on the one hand and free-form or random social discussion substitutes on the other—the student will have opportunities enough to develop both imaginative and intellectual powers. Besides the differences within a discipline, further differences between disciplines increase the chance that the student will avoid a premature freezing into any single method of thought.

However, many students today look beyond disciplines and methods of thought to some ultimate answer—their identity or perhaps the gestalt of the cosmos and their place in it. Since classroom courses seem to ignore these questions, they turn elsewhere for their answers. Even the ambitious courses that move into topics of the self and the cosmos often work on the assumption that the function of the university is to raise questions, not answer them.

It is true that if the student seeks an instant total answer in the classroom he will not get it, but neither is he likely to get it from any other source. His identity is not simply there to be found,

25

The Voiceless University

for it is still in the making; and the cosmic answer is a wisdom that comes to few among the old and to fewer still among the young. But we claim that the classroom, in our proposed form, can take him along the way and do so with some staying power.

For us to support this claim, it is necessary to look more closely at the classroom from within. We have said that the teacher develops an idea about the subject in a sustained and disciplined manner and does so as a professional. We have also said that the student participates in various ways as he learns, including his roles as judge and tester. But how can the student be a judge in an expert's field? He could be if the teacher were incompetent, but normally the teacher has much more background in the discipline than the student has. If the classroom session sticks to the subject matter, must not the student be only a receiver of what is handed out?

Many students think so and resent what they regard as the silent inferiority the classroom assigns them. Hence, they call for plan-together-as-you-go courses rather than courses concerned with an expert's preset field of knowledge.

But such formulations miss the peculiarity of the subject matter of a university classroom—at least as it ought to be. A university course does not include the whole body of knowledge of the field, although it is dependent on it (just as that whole body of knowledge of a field is not constituted of the ultimate truths of the universe, although dependent on them). Rather, a course is constituted of a finite structure of discourse, a boundable segment of a field that is in some way self-contained. It has its beginning, middle, and end *in the course,* so far as practicable. While perhaps only the expert knows how to deal the cards, he plays, and all play, with the cards on the table; and the rules of testing truth claims or value claims are open to discussion. So far as the expert's truth claims are open to testing by criteria available to the student, the student is relatively autonomous, although a follower; and the expert is dependent, although of broader knowledge. (This is also why the classroom can provide high drama if student and teacher alike are acute.)

This conception of the classroom session as an organized dis-

26

course, and of the course as a finite structure of discourses, speaks directly to the question of identity and self-expression. The student moves toward self-knowledge, not in the final sense of grasping some irreducible essence of himself, but in the more concrete sense of experiencing his own power of judgment. He evaluates truth claims and thereby discovers grounds for relying on himself as a judge. The truths acquired in such a process are peculiarly one's own, distinct from beliefs based on what others say and from ideas expressing the private feeling of the moment. What the student accepts as true, in that phase of the classroom process we are describing, he accepts not only as in accord with his private feelings now but as acceptable on grounds that have public worth. If he challenges the truth claim, he is now capable of stating reasons that are more authoritative than opinion.

A student can find no ultimate answer on his identity in this process, but the partial insight he gets into his independent powers can be clear and additive. There is a by-product in that "identity" can come to be understood not only as a globular term referring loosely to what is unique or individual about a man or group, but also to what he has or wants to have most firmly in common with other men—that is, shared grounds of judgment. The ground he employs is his own in that he can use it and does stand up for his findings. That he can defend them is what attaches them to him indissolubly. That he offers them as valid, not for himself alone but for all men, marks the common quality he shares with all men.

Apart from the fashionable question of identity, the classroom process we have described is obviously central to education. It seeks to enable the student to take responsibility for whatever he asserts to be true; the power to meet this responsibility is the mark of having learned something.

We must not overstate the student's autonomy in this process, for it is emergent, not antecedently given. The classroom provides the context of disciplined thought and the systematic content of knowledge that enable the student to develop this self-dependence. Without that classroom context, he is in danger of simply accepting random reactions. To accept or reject claims responsibly, the student obviously must first develop the kind of understanding of the subject that classroom teaching is adapted to give. Most students would not develop the base for judgment except by classroom experience. The rush to independent study is appropriate only for those whose backgrounds are sufficiently strong and whose objectives are sufficiently pointed to indicate a promise of success in what is perhaps the most lonely and difficult, though also undoubtedly the most rewarding, undertaking an individual can pursue. We feel that independent study should become a privilege for those who have shown they can best benefit by it. In order to reach this readiness, good solid classroom work is essential.

Comparable strictures apply to the search for group projects devoted to free-play interchange, in which various people toss out ideas rapidly, bounce them back and forth, and see what conclusions emerge for the individual or collectively for the group—a kind of high-pressure brainstorming. So far as such sessions seek some pointedly particular resolution to a limited problem, they are of doubtful value in the advancement of knowledge. But so far as they are not subject to such limitations, they could be immensely fruitful. That possibility is not enough, however, to recommend the process universally. The question is who the members of such a group should be. It might appear that anyone should participate, since the process is one of free play. But fruitful free play is like independent study—it is for the man with disciplined knowledge or skill. Not only would it become meaningless play for persons not properly grounded, but even if they should hit a great idea, they would have little means of recognizing it as such. The classroom system provides the structural bases that can make the impact of a new idea visible.

AUTONOMOUS IDEAS

Although we have explicitly delayed the topic of subject matter until now, it should be evident from our treatment of the preceding topics that we make it central to the classroom.

We must now ask what features the subject should have

in order to stimulate active intellectual interest and at the same time submit to the critical judgment of teacher and student alike? This question lies at the base of our whole argument—and at the heart of the intellectual life of the university. Reasonable views about it are obscured, however, by the terms in which the answer is usually discussed. For example, it is often said that for a subject-matter presentation to be stimulating, it must be concrete rather than abstract, significant rather than fact-filled. We disagree and maintain that abstract discourse can generate intense, sustained interest, as in mathematics; and the factual discourse of history can magnetize listeners.

What is it that can give life to purposive discourse and abstract reasoning? One kind of answer is that abstractions can tie in with other ideas, can be used in varied applications, and can suggest new ideas. This kind of explanation seems valid to us but not attentive enough to the relation between the idea or discourse and the mind of the person thinking it. That is, an idea is treated in these explanations as if it were some sort of object the mind works with, an identifiable entity somehow located *in* the mind of the thinker. Such a rhetorical separation of mind and idea is misleading, for the argument tends to picture the mind as the dynamic force and to relegate the ideas to the status of entities being inspected and manipulated. A more fruitful approach—and one closer to the nature of thought as experienced—is to recognize mind and idea as basically the same; the discourse or idea is itself a *piece of mind,* capable of the dynamic, logical powers that we otherwise attribute only to the mind. When one recalls an absorbing intellectual experience, one cannot separate mind from idea within it; one cannot abstract a live, moving mind from a passive idea being moved.

We neglect this fusion of idea and mind too readily. For example, we think of the sentences "p implies the sentence q" and "p is true" as two independent propositions. As such they are not connected. We then leave it to the mind to link them up in the obvious way so as to conclude "therefore q is true." This conception of how the conclusion is reached allows one to assume that the abstractness of the set of propositions makes them inert. But the first

29

two propositions, taken together as a piece of mind, clearly are directed to the establishment of q's truth value: "therefore q" is the completion of the idea inherent in the propositions. To grasp the idea is to grasp this inner continuity. To make the same point by a less fanciful metaphor: such an idea is *autonomous*—that is, it is literally a law unto itself.

The propositions above possessed a simple ideational continuity, but complicated ideas and discourses can also have an inherent line of development. The development can vary in method —deductive, inductive, dialectical, and so on—according to which movement is required by, and proper to, the idea. For example, it suited Newton's purpose to present his theory as the methodological consequence of basic laws, while Watson chose to show that his theory of the double helix is inherent in otherwise unorganized data. However, both scientists exhibited the intellectual achievement as self-moving and self-justifying.

Our point is also of general application to subject matter; it works with a limerick no less than a theory of motion. Consider the following:

> *There was a young man from Japan*
> *Whose verses never would scan.*
> *When told this was so,*
> *He said, "Yes, I know,"*

These four lines are heavy with what is to come—and with criteria by which to judge whether it is satisfactory when it does come. Our mind, like the poem, awaits the completion of the rhythm and the meaning. Here is the ending: "But I like to make the last line as long as I possibly can." Clearly the fun is in the way the poem itself both makes this newborn line illegitimate and at the same time legitimates it. In generating and applying its own power of legitimation and illegitimation the poem becomes an autonomous idea.

We stress two supportive reasons for the centrality of the classroom in the educational process. The first is the one already made—that here knowledge most authentically comes alive, making the distinction between feeling and reasoning trivial. Even the mathematician in class can be "possessed," not because he has some volatile spirits bubbling in him as he looks at the inert proof on the blackboard, but because the proof is itself internally alive and unfolding itself. The second consequence concerns the basis for judging the adequacy of arguments and truth claims when these are made, as they should be in the normal university classroom, in connection with the autonomous idea they are bound up with. In that case, a significant basis of judgment is provided by a grasp of the line of continuity inherent in the idea. As a student moves closer to a grasp of an idea, he also comes closer to the point at which an invalid conclusion ("therefore not q") will be as unacceptable to him as would a comic ending to *King Lear*.

Here then is the explanation—and the source—of the student's power in the classroom to pass reasoned verdicts with confidence: they are grounded not simply in his receptiveness to what is presented nor in his responses to the stimuli of the presentation, but in his participation in the push and motion—the autonomous life—of the discourse. The teacher requires the feedback in turn because the discourse is being tested not simply as a piece of his private mind but as a piece of man's mind.

Of course, ideas and talk can be directionless, and therefore dead, whether abstract or concrete, emotive or rational, discussional or dogmatic. An idea comes alive not simply through a here-and-now sparkle; it lives only if it has a life line, an inherent pattern of development. This inherent life of the idea, we argue, is central to the university classroom and is the reason the classroom is in turn central to the educational process at the highest levels of pre-professional and liberal thought.

A student overzealous in his attacks on depersonalization in the curriculum rose at a recent meeting and disparaged the importance of reading books. He could not have personal interaction or give-and-take with the dry printed word. Moreover, he said, the book was written for faceless men, not for him as a unique individual. We are altogether in sympathy with the young man's search for vital contact but would suggest that he misses the point: the living process he seeks is in books as structures of language, although it may require a classroom to make them intellectually visible to him. The classroom is organized by the same kind of dynamic structures that organize books (whether dialogue, inquiry, or memoir—the variety of kinds of structure of language is equally great in books and class). Thus, there is a natural affinity between them; classes and books are extensions of each other.

John Milton wrote: ". . . books are not absolutely dead things, but do contain a potency of life in them to be as active as that soul whose progeny they are . . . a good book is the precious life-blood of a master spirit, embalmed and treasured up on purpose to a life beyond life."[3] The way Milton characterizes the structure of language is more felicitous, of course, than our characterization of it as a piece of living mind, but our point follows his, and we echo his warning that we had "as good almost kill a man as kill a good book." What we argue is that the classroom can or should go furthest in the educational process to prevent such deaths, for its nature is to seek to generate what Milton calls a "life beyond life."

[3] John Milton, "Areopagitica," *The Complete Poetry and Selected Prose* (Modern Library), p. 681.

Knowledge, Power, and Community

 3

Students assert that the central problem in universities today is how the institutions will be governed. On the other hand, administrators maintain that the major problem is how the universities can accommodate the needs of the new variety of students. Thus, while the administration is concerned about accommodating more students, the students wish to take over administrative responsibility. These two views of the problem may help us locate what the problem really is.

We start with those who hold that the old system is run by old men who have little understanding of youths and their needs. Presumably, the power structure or Establishment maintains tight autocratic control over our universities, and this control must be broken in order to restructure the system according to the real educational needs of the students. The argument maintains that as presently constituted, the institutions are instruments used by those in power to maintain the present system and feed new personnel into the system to play their appointed roles. Further, the origins of the educational institutions in our country are taken as proof that they are designed to extend the interest and influence of other institutions in our society—namely, the church, the state, the city, and business or technical organizations.

The Voiceless University

The power analysis of contemporary problems in higher education is essentially neo-Marxian in the sense that it emphasizes the conflicts among groups or classes. Such analysis acquires credibility when public officials insist that the solution to student unrest is simply a matter of law enforcement, thus proving that society is ready to impose its will upon the academic world. Even within universities, both use of force to maintain order and accession to student demands under demeaning conditions of violence or threats of violence give additional credence to the power analysis of the situation. All participants accept the students' belief that the problem is essentially one of power or control, although they differ about where the focus of power should be.

Within the university, group confrontations have spread from students against the administration to students confronting faculty, faculty at odds with the administration, and younger radical faculty opposed to older tenured faculty. Under these circumstances, older faculty sometimes attempt to identify with students to avoid potential difficulties. And conversely, sometimes younger faculty conceal their beliefs (and half-way apologize for their long hair that identifies them with student activists) in the fear that such identifications may adversely affect personnel decisions. Even when younger faculty defiantly flaunt their identification with activists, little is added to the academic situation.

Others have attempted to explain the present situation in different non-Marxist terms. For example, Edward Shils traces youth unrest to the pampered permissive feelings generated in an affluent society—Society of Plenitude—where their desires are readily and immediately satisfied. Such accounts do reveal interesting psychological and social aspects of the total situation, but they are not operative—that is, effective as grounds for action in the university—whereas the neo-Marxist analysis is pointed to action. Our concern, however, is not to account for student unrest, but rather to understand how universities allowed student unrest to become channeled in the way it has developed. Even if all the theories about student unrest are correct, it is more important to understand the failure in universities' operations that allowed oppositionist

34

causes to come into play so easily and with such unfortunate effects. We leave to Chapter Six the question of the formal problems of a governing structure for a university and here examine the kind of structure that has evolved in universities as appropriate for their functioning. It appears that the very looseness of structure, so necessary for a university to do its job, may well also be the major condition that has allowed oppositionist causes to thrive with their unfortunate effects. But let us turn now to the administrator's conceptions of the major problems in universities today.

COMMUNICATION GAP

The view of the universities' problems held by responsible officials emphasizes the great influx of students from widely different backgrounds (in many cases from families that previously had no contact with universities), with widely varying goals (in many cases unformulated), and in an atmosphere affected by racial problems and a limited and senseless war. The open-admissions policies and the expansion of extension programs for all interested adults have raised questions about what kinds of programs are appropriate to universities or can be maintained at proper university levels. Universities in the past have responded to the needs of society without undue stress, and there seems to be little reason why they cannot again meet these challenges. In the present case, however, the loose structure of universities, along with confrontation of groups allowed by this structure, taken in conjunction with these new social challenges, has indeed caused stress.

The administrative view has an advantage over views of the neo-Marxians, sociologists, and others in that it comes to grips with a problem that immediately and overtly confronts the university. However, all these views share one feature: they make their analysis by going to problems derived from concepts and situations that are operative in the university but peripheral to the heart of its activity as a university. Let us return to our point of focus—that is, that the single simple core of university activity is the class session. From this perspective, the interests of all groups in the university make up an essentially indivisible complex, for although their func-

35

tions differ, they converge in a common intellectual enterprise. What we have missed is a clear focus on the indivisibility of these interests; it has been co-opted by an unhealthy exaggeration of the importance of the differences in function. The chief danger in this sort of exaggeration is that it tends to translate these differences into terms of power—that is, there is a focus on constituencies rather than functions. Controversy then develops over the representation to which each constituency is entitled in university governance, and the conception of the discreteness of each group rigidifies.

No doubt one cause of this rigidification is that the actual working relationship of the groups has deteriorated and lost sight of its potential. The difficulty is primarily one of rhetoric and communication—the communication gap. This gap cannot be attributed to the traditional difference between young and old. We must look to what is missing in the training and expectation of the vast majority of the student population today. This youth claims to have instant correct intuitions of the situation as inherently divisive, and the faculty—who could contradict this assumption—remains largely silent. This communication gap is often noted, but it is usually conceived imprecisely. The emphasis is often on the lack of social or personal contact among students, faculty, and administrators, as if the solution could be found in the elimination of unfriendly distances. Such an approach has led to frenetic attempts by all groups to reestablish contacts of all kinds—especially the informal, social, and personal contacts that presumably cement a community of scholars at smaller institutions of higher learning. There is certainly nothing wrong with such distance-cutting activities, and in individual cases, students, instructors, and administrators may learn something helpful and enhance the enjoyment of their work. Yet the lack of social contacts could hardly have been a major source of student unrest.

The nature of a communication gap becomes clear only when the focus of communication—or lack of communication—is clearly spelled out. We see the failure to be in communicating what the idea of a university is. At the specific level, it takes the form of a professional communication gap. It begins in the classroom (as indicated in Chapter Two) when the process is so restricted or mechanical that it does not exhibit what professional activity and experience are. The gap extends from that initial void to the broader dimensions of university life. Here, especially, there is presently a failure of the professionals to communicate—and to modify from feedback—an understanding of this larger life of the university bound up with or derivative from disciplined inquiry.

Our discussion, therefore, must move to the system of values operative peculiarly, or paradigmatically, in a university community. The basic elements perhaps seem conspicuously self-evident. Despite some frustrations, the values far outweigh the attendant dissatisfactions. One younger faculty member indicated his amazement at actually being paid to read books, to talk with others about common problems, and to think about problems he enjoyed working on. Yet this formulation is too loose, for the system of values upon which it stands is not self-evident to students today. This lack of understanding may be the occasion or condition that has made disruptions possible, although it is hardly a motivating cause. The loose university structure with the influx of students who have previously had no contact with or ideas about the values constituting a university does indeed present a problem of a professional communication gap.

Many faculty members today face this new situation with either of two opinions: universities as they previously existed are doomed to extinction, or they will be preserved only in special institutions or special honors programs for the elite students. We argue that the relevant features about a university community can be communicated to fill the professional communication gap, that awareness of these features constitutes a basis for understanding the knowledge/power problems found in current internal and external campus problems, and that these defeatist and elitist opinions about the future of universities are false.

ACTIVITY OF IDEAS

To talk of university life, we must always begin with the teaching-learning relationship, which is clearly based on sharing in the evolution of a common structure of ideas. Accordingly, university life, broadly conceived, is best understood in terms of the rich variety of modes of ideational sharing extending beyond the classroom. The pursuit of a common problem by teams of researchers within the same segment of a field is a paradigmatic case. The way in which this pursuit can become the life style of a group is indicated clearly in James Watson's account of the double helix. Although the scientific search for solutions is the main drive, the activity is also intensely competitive, as exemplified in Watson's rivalry with Linus Pauling to be the discoverer of the solution. But they still share a common goal, for a team's success is achieved by attaining universal agreement about the solution to the given problem—especially the agreement of its strongest rival. This agreement marks the fundamental sharing of knowledge-oriented criteria of judgment as distinct from power-oriented votes or protests from constituencies.

Some would argue that consensus in this case is little different from a political decision by the majority, since the allocation of rewards and the commitment of resoures is determined by what the dominant voice says, whether it be the voice of most scientists approving a theory or of most citizens approving a decision. This interesting theoretical question deserves discussion in university life, but for our purposes it is enough to note that the scientific consensus cannot claim legitimacy by citing the count but only by citing the proof, while the democratic consensus cannot claim legitimacy by citing the proof but only the count.

As relations branch out to different segments or schools of a particular discipline, political byplay appears to have some significance; and students are predisposed to seize on this kind of politics as the center of academic affairs. This problem will not be solved until the appointment of a philosopher king, but certain tempering facts should be noted: the paradigm remains the working team centered on ideas, and the conflicts of departmental politics often have to be waged in the form of intellectual tournaments. Again, the power-jockeying, say for control of a new appointment, takes place on the foundation of a wide consensus on credentials and evidence of intellectual standing and achievement in a field, so that the region within which the tournament is fought is quite narrow. Finally, faculty who focus on the political goals rather than the intellectual are usually destined to play secondary supporting roles to those whose academic achievement has brought them leadership in the community.

Filling the professional communication gap is not merely a matter of describing and appraising activities outside the student's immediate ken, however. There are important areas of faculty concern that are not directly taught but are relevant to students seeking the implications of a focus on the maintenance, advancement, and dissemination of knowledge. Inquiry into and teaching of some aspects of a field—biology, mathematics, sociology—have larger implications for the total structure of such fields of knowledge. Today, for example, the sociological analysis of business organizations must take account of their interaction with the community—their ecology, as it were. Such knowledge adds qualitatively to the student's—and the faculty's—theoretical conception of the field, for instead of being seen as a given body of knowledge to which additions may be made, the need and possibility of the new development become part of the intelligible structure of the field. Again, the students become aware of the options in the field. The implications of even a limited inquiry must be envisaged in terms of practical consequences—first, to the university itself and, second, to the social processes outside it.

Finally, university life involves a sharing of ideas at a level or form common to the whole community, for all segments of the community are each other's potential public. In such activities as public lectures in diverse fields, the performing arts, and social action, the university life can be a model for any community; it can be a model of diversity and openness. Also, there is an analogy between the relation of teacher and student on the one hand and the performing artist or lecturer and his audience on the other. Just as in a classroom the functions of expert and student are indivisible, so also in the concert hall or public lecture, the functioning of a great audience is also required. A good audience responds not on the basis of random private taste but on the basis of developed critical power to judge what falls within its areas of taste.

A sign of the professional communication gap is visible in the kinds of activities students tend to sponsor today in the performing arts and public speech. Instead of the diversity one would expect from the broad range of pursuits of university life, there is an amazing uniformity—the avant-garde art form and the liberal-to-radical headliner dominate the field. Instead of a plurality of heterogeneous events, each with some audience, there tends to be a greater disparity between the mass-drawing features and the less fashionable events.

We recognize that a number of facets of university life we have noted are noted by others—we have sought in part to reinforce them, but our focus has been on the way in which apparently disparate aspects of a university community hang together when seen as variants and extensions of the relationship made central in the classroom as it ought to be.

CONSEQUENCES FOR CAMPUS PROBLEMS

Peaceful conditions generally, and the autonomy of intellectual activities individually, are required by the nature of the university. This is a truism. But two aspects of it are not sufficiently stressed.

Nations require peace, as do universities. But for better or worse the power to wage war is part of the makeup of a nation and waging war in defense of the integrity of the nation is natural, although maintaining peace and national integrity is certainly more desirable. But disruptions of peace are essentially unnatural in a university community. It may be asked: are there no grievances, however sore and otherwise irremediable, that warrant disruption? We are tempted to answer "None!" For universities are peculiarly free of power factors in their aim and structure. There is no coercion of membership; students are free to withdraw from classes, programs, or whole institutions and to seek a different atmosphere at another institution. And further, the effectiveness of nondisruptive demonstrations may be much greater than impatient persons

40

are willing to entertain. There appears to have been little imaginative use of the possibilities of peaceful action, for people seem to be eager for the more newsworthy type of demonstration. Finally, disruptive demonstrations seem justified in a university only when peaceful demonstrations are outlawed—and at such time, they constitute a last resort against a great and immediate threat. When such a threat obtains, and police power has invaded the campus, the university has virtually ceased to exist. In this sense, justified disruptive demonstrations are not directed against the university but against its suppressors.

The Marcusean claim that the cultural atmosphere is suppressive hardly qualifies here. Indeed, the fact that Marcuse sees the need to claim that Establishment attitudes and peaceful procedures for dissent are equivalent to physical inhibition admits the force of our argument; for he in effect concedes that unless he can show that peaceful procedures are like police coercion, he has no valid objection to them. Our more straightforward position is that disruptive demonstrations are not justifiable in a university unless the law or police preclude peaceful ones, because it is especially in a university that the possibilities of persuasion should not be sold short.

The other point not sufficiently stressed pertains to the necessity for autonomy in university activities, such as research. The ultimate ground for autonomy is not the right of each researcher to do as he pleases, as a right analogous to those in the Bill of Rights and as an academic civil liberty. It is that, of course. But the ultimate ground of the autonomy is that it is intellectual. The focus is not on power but on knowledge, not on having a right to do something but on being qualified to do it well.

How does the idea of the university as a community based on shared ideas in a heterogeneous professional context bear on current campus problems? Many faculty members have become concerned with the extended responsibilities implied by their special areas of competence and are now rethinking, reformulating, and re-presenting these implications to the newer participants in university life. The effort is piecemeal and tedious but nonetheless

41

important. Further, the focus of disciplined thought on finite problems ties in with this kind of effort.

The same argument-by-argument method applies to other campus problems—such as curriculum, governance, drugs, and race. Only by such a piecemeal approach to each set of problems can the normal processes of university operation be reconstituted in the face of the globular revolutionary criticism. Whether it be Ralph Nader attacking the automotive industry about safety or biologists using judicial procedures to protect our environment from pollution, piecemeal attacks on evils really solve problems. The university's autonomy is a necessary condition for the free inquiry that enables this piecemeal criticism to have an effect on society. And the universities alone can produce the critical analysis by which they can solve their own problems. The primary responsibility for this activity rests with those who are skilled at constructing piecemeal arguments appropriate to specific problems at hand—that is, the members of the faculty. But the self-criticism must be shared by all participants in a university. Hope for increasingly effective results rests on this self-criticism, which may reveal the inadequacies of the revolutionary mode of thought before it leads to disruptive actions. The contrast between the use of piecemeal arguments and of the globular approach is directly related to our discussion of knowledge and power. Whereas the user of the globular method already knows the answer and so can progress only by the use of power, the person using the piecemeal approach proceeds empirically and analytically.

We said that members of the faculty were most eligible to make these arguments—but which faculty? One approach suggests that for each problem there are relevant experts; for example, the drug problem can be approached in various ways by psychologists, sociologists, lawyers, and medical doctors. Of course, we would enlist the experts, since the push of our argument is to restore recognition of neglected dimensions of expertise, but there are reasons to spread the responsibility. Some campus problems take on their character not simply from the psychological-medical factors for drugs or from political factors for governance but also from the nature of university life and decision making. Therefore, we want experts with shared knowledge of the nature of a university community, as well as with specific professional knowledge.

These arguments by no means negate the effectiveness of the day-to-day classroom sessions; rather they are extensions of such sessions that are meant to respond to the attacks upon the university. As such, their ultimate effectiveness depends primarily upon the effectiveness of the basic classroom activity and course development. Arguments supporting the autonomy of knowledge and the activities involving its acquisition and dissemination must ultimately be based upon its continued acquisition and dissemination—an indispensable circularity. Without this continuity the revolutionary attack can carry the battle simply because it interrupts the fundamental university activity.

ROLES OF KNOWLEDGE AND POWER

We have already discussed some dimensions of knowledge as it is grounded in specialized disciplines and in awareness of the pervasive values of university life. In a later chapter we explore the ways in which the student's knowledge of what he studies and of the university's significance to him can affect the operations of the institution. Here we wish to turn to the locus of authority—society —that seems most distinct from the workings of knowledge.

Since society provides the money and legitimates the authority of the university, society mandates the ends to be achieved; there has to be some coincidence between the ends thus grounded in society's desires and the ends pursued by members of the university. But the power/knowledge distinction here is not nearly so sharp as indicated, for power unsupported by knowledge is inarticulate. Society specifies ends only generally, as a normal procedure. (Even when society breaks the norm and prescribes specific actions, it only knows how to act on persons or particular books, not on structures of ideas as such. It may want this man fired or that book banned but then runs out of words and plans.) The purposes served by the university receive their concreteness and specification, not in society's mandates, but in the formulations and processes set up by knowledge-oriented faculty; this is the case whether one speaks of society as establishing a medical school or encouraging the liberal arts. The medical faculty structures the medical school; the liberal arts faculty structures its curriculum. It should be understood that we are not setting up two disparate entities—society and the university—for all members of the latter are in the former, and an increasing proportion of society has ties with the university; the distinction is rather between the roles of knowledge and of political power. Each is sovereign in its sphere, and our goal is to point out the legitimate and harmonious manner in which the university can enter into that relation and yet properly maintain the sovereignty of knowledge.

There are two kinds of knowledge that function to maintain and implement public support of the university. The first is the public understanding of the necessity for the existence of universities in society not merely to provide the technical information for industrial-commercial activity but primarily to encourage the inquiry and criticism that lead society to improve itself. As citizens, participants in the university also join in the formulation of this public understanding; and, as members of the university community, they bear special responsibility for contributions to it.

The second type is the knowledge and understanding possessed by boards of regents and the top administrative officers charged with carrying out the mandate of the public. They are concerned with adapting means to ends in contexts in which appropriate separation of functions according to knowledge possessed is duly achieved and the rights and obligations of individual participants are appropriately protected and exacted. But since the ends are in large measure determined autonomously by the faculty, and since most administrative officers are chosen from among the faculty, there is clear overlap of functions between faculty and administration in addition to the general identity of interest of all groups in the university in maintaining the essential university activities—teaching and learning.

In the interplay of these various groups and officials exercising various kinds of expertise and authority, differences of judgment about particular issues inevitably occur. Such differences are not a cause of difficulty when the appropriate relations of knowledge and power are maintained. Difficulty arises when the differences are cast into the form of confrontation of power blocs, and such crisis situations are encouraged and reinforced when the universities are organized in terms of "appropriate" representation of power blocs. A primary need then is to avoid power-bloc organizations and the theories that support them. Of course, any devices that can minimize the deleterious effect of such organizations without affecting the educational processes should be used: the publication of all information that will not adversely affect individual careers or general personnel operations, the public deliberations on curriculum, and so on. But such devices are clearly ancillary and are needed to help reestablish the trust necessary for satisfactory university operations. They cannot replace the central educational processes themselves, which are ultimately the sources from which all such devices arise and are justified.

In sum, then, the relations of internal knowledge and external power in the operations of the university are complex, but the complexity exists to create a fair chance for knowledge to maintain its autonomous function in a socially valuable and valued university.

COMMUNITY OF COMMUNITIES

We argued earlier that the university community is based on the sharing of ideas and the activities centered on the discovery, development, and experiential embodiments of these ideas. This base gives the university its link with society, since all human and social processes—from house building to theater going to war and peace—are idea based. The university must also preserve its distinct knowledge orientation in its pursuit of ideas. To preserve both its distinctness and its universality, the university must function as a community of communities—that is, as a community distinct from those advocated by two less pluralistic views widely held today, the elitist and the spontaneist views.

The elitist focuses on the theoretical purity and depth of

the intellectual's concerns. This intellectuality for him gives university life its true distinctness and fits it exclusively for the elite. The elitist is dismayed by the descent upon the university of an ever-higher percentage of the nation's young, with the demand for open admissions. He wants the university to set up pragmatically viable programs (vocational training and entertainment) for the greater number of students, while reserving genuinely higher education in honors programs and higher institutes for the elite.

The elitist purports to be defending the integrity of intellectual disciplines, but in fact he is insensitive to their versatility. The lengthening of the time period of education of youth, while it involves psychological difficulties, still constitutes a remarkable opportunity to lift the level and quality of life of these youths in their adulthood. But we lose much of the chance to exploit this great opportunity if we freeze the conception of worthwhile intellecual activity at the institute level.

Plato is often accused of being a slave-grinding aristocrat. But on a notable occasion, when he wished to show the basic nature of intellectual activity, he called in Meno's slave boy. The boy did more than take in what Socrates said; he *judged* its validity as a proof of the Pythagorean theorem (of which he had never heard). Socrates accordingly used the slave's experience as a model of how man's mind succeeds by thought. Compatible with this view is the view neglected by the elitists that the classroom is the place where the minds of the young begin to work, not as instruments in the formation of habits or as idiosyncratically immature mechanisms, but as minds capable of autonomous judgments. The universality of this capacity—although in varying levels—provides a base as solid as granite for meeting the new challenge and opportunity.

The tendency to rigidify the distinction between the elite and the mass has an extreme, albeit a benevolent, form in B. F. Skinner's *Walden II,* where everyone does as he pleases. But there is a community of scientists (psychologists) engaged in research on the remaking of man, a team intended to be a "super-organism" of the new society. However, this special group is but a variant of the wise-man doctrine that we dismissed in Chapter Two as not only inapplicable to the present circumstances of 7 million students, but also as theoretically false to the nature of the knowledge to be taught; for it professes to rise above the plurality of subject matters in a way that levels out significant differences between them.

Even when the elitist view allows for the diversity of experts, nonetheless the availability of their expertise to other members of the community tends to be lost. But, as illustrated by Meno's slave boy, there is much that can be done below the institute level. First, the number of the young who could make critical contact with a subject at a preprofessional level is much greater than the number who will want, or be able, to go all the way with the subject; the difference, that is, is in level *not* in generic ability. Second, the principle of autonomous ideas is not restricted to the more abstract subject matters but can be applied to most subjects capable of being taught; indeed, the teachability of a subject, as we treated it in Chapter Two, is just its susceptibility to such development. Third, as indicated earlier in this chapter, the principle of great publics or great audiences for the work of expert and artist, in popular form, rests on the necessary translatability of ideas into the experience of the literate nonexpert.

The elitist view makes of the university two disparate communities. Ours makes of it a community of these communities. There is a need for institutes and for lower-level training. But the points of contact we have emphasized—the conditions of disciplined inquiry, the experiential form of ideas and, above all, the way all activities of the mind can exhibit a recognizably common humanity—are all based on a *sharing* of ideas, and without sharing there is no community.

At the opposite pole from the elitist view is the spontaneist view, which makes all the young eligible for—indeed determinative of—true university life. Ortega y Gasset argues that each generation must discover its own life style, and the university is where the young today are building their counterculture based on the values of uninhibited intuitions and following one's own inclinations. Since society outside the university is hostile to this effort, the university is where the young can shape this life style in readiness for the day when they become society.

This view, even more than the elitist, misses the sense of the university as a community of communities. The spontaneist, although committed to individuality, has tended to produce a generally uniform life. We do not speak of uniform modes of hair and dress but of standards of taste, sources of satisfaction, and political slogans. More important, the modes of sharing these pursuits are not like the sharing in a structure of ideas; rather the new modes seem to be flattening out. For example, "discussions" become progressively difficult to distinguish from the mass rally that presents a sequence of short chant-provoking speakers. The irony of Marcuse's call for self-expression as a way of making man two-dimensional is that in the relative sanctuary of the dormitory, where external society has little impact, there is a tendency toward a single dimension.

We would defend the spontaneist against the conventional kind of criticism, for the cause of uniformity is not that youth only wants to conform. The spontaneist *is* trying to be individual, to express himself, and would be content perhaps if the mark of his rapport with others was their recognition of his unique mode of expression.

The difficulty lies in the absence of the ideational content or sources of diversity that are the true centers of university life. It is hard to get diversity out of little or no content; interests diversify only as pursued problems and subjects diversify. And when a given interest is complex, groupings or subcommunities can form around it in a way that enhances rather than threatens the individuality of each member.

In order for such groupings or subcommunities to form a larger community, it is not enough that each group respect the right of others to do whatever they please. This approach soon ceases to be respect and becomes a vacuous or uncomprehending tolerance. The respect that grounds community in diversity is some kind of mutual understanding among those following different pursuits, its basis being the recognition of the common concern with disciplined pursuits.

In sum, the spontaneist's view blurs respect for the integrity of ideas, and the elitist's view lacks recognition of their place in the minds of all men. Our view finds most men can engage in and appreciate the force of ideas, although such appreciation is not superficial self-expression of momentary impulses. Further, development of such pervasive human capacity is essential for a cohesive democratic society.

Student Idealism
in a
World of Overkill

 4

The idea of the university is necessarily bound up with the idealism of youth, but there are simplified and contrasting views of what the connection is and what it should be. One view is that the university has no role beyond that of furnishing space for discussions, just as it provides space for chess clubs; another is that the university must embark on social-action programs or disruptive protests in local communities and on the national scene. In this chapter it is necessary first to examine the social context and then seek within the university for the features relevant to it.

Society's ills are manifold; the variety defies man's imagination. Even if we restrict our attention to suffering inflicted upon innocent children, the list seems endless: their starvation in Biafra; their stunted growth in city slums and migrant-worker camps; their subjection to cruel beatings and death in increasing numbers by their own parents. Beyond these ills, we find innumerable other deficiencies, the most prominent being, of course, wars (in Vietnam and the Middle East), racial injustice, and neglected poverty. These problems among others have been at the center of attention of various universities and their students and have been the major apparent causes for demonstrations in universities today—against ROTC, against investments in South Africa by private universities,

50

against infringement of universities on surrounding slums, and so on.

But there are even more frightening ills for mankind. Unrestrained nuclear war could eliminate all life on this planet. And we are becoming increasingly aware that poisonous hydrocarbons are upsetting the delicate biological balance upon which life is maintained. Other possibilities for air and water pollution through industrial and human waste and garbage abound. Even the fertility of the human species threatens to overpopulate our planet as it is despoiled and made incapable of supporting life. There is an even more devastating fact about these greater dangers; they are subject to man's control, yet apparently nothing or little is being done to insure that the human race or even all life on earth will survive them. Professor Wald, the famous biologist, pointed to these deep-seated ills as the ultimate motives for student unrest and demonstrations. Many believe that the next generation has no future or a future with dangers of a magnitude never before faced by men. Young idealists view the probability of human self-destruction with rage and resentment toward their conventionally minded elders whose stupidity has apparently cut short the life expectations of the species.

The most obvious and healthy response of our youth must be a move to action in the face of such danger. The well-known idealism of youth makes this move the most obvious and most rational one under the circumstances. Recent commentators have praised the vigor and idealism of our youth as our best hope for an improved society. They have indeed echoed Aristotle's insight into the character of the young. "Youth would always rather do noble deeds than useful ones: their lives are regulated more by moral feeling than by reasoning; and whereas reasoning leads us to choose what is useful, moral goodness leads us to choose what is noble."[1] But Aristotle misses the main point that what is noble is also useful in this case and that the moral feeling of youth appears to be combined with a simple and direct reasoning based on a calculation of a short human life expectancy.

[1] *Rhetoric*, Bk. II, Ch. 12.

The Voiceless University

In addition, a portion of our society has sensitized our youth to their obligation to others, even as other portions create the situations so desperately requiring remedies. We criticize callous people for their lack of humanitarian sensitivity. We condemned individuals who did not call the police while a man killed a woman on the street below a New York City apartment complex, and we condemned a whole nation when 6 million Jews were murdered in Germany without noticeable protest. Thus, the normal idealism of youth has been reinforced by a socially generated sense of guilt in many of the most sensitive and intelligent youths in our society. Since both the elements of corruption and the sources of criticism are present, we should not then be astonished that youths today are so ready to rebel against the deficiencies of our society and of the world.

The rebels have not given up. They are willing to take desperate action and to accept great personal risk in order to right the wrongs they find around them. For them, the ills are obvious; talk has not produced any solution; in fact, talk only prolongs the ills; the time for action is *now*. And the action required is indeed radical.

REVOLUTIONARY, IDEALISTIC VIEW

Radicals argue that the various deficiencies in our society are primarily symptoms of the sickness of the whole society and that only a complete revolution can cure our ills. Thus, their goal is to overthrow the Establishment and to replace it with a structure sensitive to the real needs of the people. Further, they hold that the ills of society infect our universities and make them into instruments of the established institutions of society. Thus, the disruption of the universities seems to them a logical first step in a general social revolution. To this end, they court violent police confrontations or engage in guerilla tactics as a means of enlisting support from hitherto uncommitted students, thus hastening the day of revolution.

The radicals' goals are only vaguely and negatively defined by their use of the term "freedom": freedom from restraint, freedom to act as they wish only within the restriction that such action not hurt others, freedom from economic and political oppression, freedom available equally to all men. The intricate mechanisms that have evolved to help maintain even the modicum of freedom we now know constitute unwanted restrictions to them. The vast literature arguing the complexities of such notions as freedom and the necessities of law, responsibility, and accountability, the organization of society and the devices necessary for persons to live together in peace and relative harmony, are for the radical all irrelevant talk designed to confuse what is obvious and immediate.

The pain and suffering attendant upon all revolutions, even when successful, appear as necessary evils to attain the ultimate goal of a better world. But the revolutionaries here neglect the evidence of history. In a society that provides legal modes of solving problems, total revolution produces greater ills than those which occasioned it. The revolutionaries even believe it is necessary to precipitate severe repression; they accept the creation of a police state as a necessary means to their end. The horrible realities of a police state make the dreamlike sequence of the Hegelian dialectic— even when modified by Marx, Marcuse, and others—indeed most idealistic. The prospects for realizing the ideal thus carries within itself a notion of its opposite with no assurance that the dream sequence will be completed. This possibility alone suggests to us that disruptive demonstrations or guerilla activities undertaken with the goal of generating revolution are clearly not the best or even a likely solution for the nation's problems.

But the basis for rejection of the revolutionary approach is made stronger when one recognizes the fact that universities have their own goals and activities for which any adequate society must provide the appropriate free conditions. If the ends and activities of universities can indeed be shown to be a source of attaining a better society, then the revolutionary, idealistic view must be rejected on that ground as well as on the ground that it depends on a speculative and regressive logic of events.

The university is an arena in which conflicting ideas are supported and opposed by argument. The same ideas outside the university may well become driving forces behind programs and campaigns involving the use of political or other kinds of power. Even though the same person who defends and develops the idea intellectually within the university may employ it politically outside the university, the two kinds of treatment are, or ought to be, different. Because the intellectual mode of confrontation in the university is at least briefly abstracted from the political, the university makes possible the freedom of inquiry which in the long run reshapes political institutions. Engagement in this process imposes on the proponent of any idea or institution the obligation to justify himself in argument, and thus the most venerable and also the most revolutionary conceptions of ideals underlying our actional disputes can be put to the test. In these processes, neither party has any resource except the adequacy of his research and the cogency of his argument. For this reason, the university is a necessary thorn in the side of all who would rigidify either the existing social structure or the bases for overthrowing it. Society should assure the university's autonomy for the sake of this intellectually unsettling effect on the Establishment no less than on the revolutionary.

Although we think it essential to reject the revolutionists' approach, it is nonetheless important to note several reasonable features in it. First, the unthinking response to radical demonstrations of insensitive administrators, politicians, and police has supplied the radicals with their most effective arguments and given some slight substance to the Hegelian dream sequence. Second, the revolutionary mode of action contains much that is positive, even when it also does some damage. It is vastly preferable to the fanatical and nihilistic idealistic mode of response, which rejects all aspects of life as parts of this morally tainted world and thus occasions senseless symbolic gestures such as the flaming suicide of a university youth at the United Nations building in protest against the Biafran situation. The third is a paradox. The revolutionists' push for a better life and society reveals the evils of the results that his mode of response will certainly entail. A desire to avoid those ills may ultimately engage even the revolutionaries in a more fruitful mode of action. Fourth, although the revolutionist would push for a total and comprehensive overhaul, his mode of action must take account of others who might be attracted to his side, and consequently, he must seek limited issues upon which to focus his point of attack.

AIMS OF DEMONSTRATIONS

Traditionally, students have demonstrated for many reasons from protesting poor food in the cafeteria and bad accommodations to protesting parietal hours in the dormitories. These demonstrations are palpably in the students' self-interest. Today, such expressions of self-interest have been expanded to include protest against nonstudents controlling student life and behavior, against curriculum restrictions, against university governance without student participation, against unpopular university personnel decisions, against university expansion into areas used or lived in by poor nonwhites, against ROTC, against military or war-industry recruitment on campus, against war-related research, against racial discrimination or investment (by private schools) in business in racially organized nations.

These aims are all stated negatively, against certain university actions or omissions, and they are all specific. At this level of expression, most issues can be solved within the confines of the university itself, although different campuses will arrive at different specific modes of solution. On some campuses there has been little change, while on others students have obtained primary control over permissible behavior (except where the local and state laws apply against them), relaxation of curriculum restrictions, a voice in university governance and representation on various committees, modification of university action on surrounding areas, elimination of ROTC, abolition of secret research contracts, and positive gains for strengthening the representation of minority groups on campuses.

The various degrees of student success in these matters show that the issues and their outcome contain diverse elements whose worth varies for the universities. Most changes of this sort presumably have value in that they involve students in internal affairs of the university. The business of the university may move more slowly, but the involvement may also offer an educational opportunity to those who participate in the process. Students may learn the difficulties of joint decision making in a common enterprise of persons whose professional knowledges are so diverse. The students may also be better prepared to understand the differences between this process and politics of the community, state, or nation. But such considerations are of major interest only to those primarily interested in the social sciences. A determination of the educational value of such activity for students in the social sciences is hardly possible and possibly trivial (how much credit should accrue for such activity?). For those not in the social sciences, such activity may have only peripheral value and may even divert them from other activities more important to their educational aims.

Some changes involving the relations of the university to society (such as secret government research contracts or ROTC) are clearly good if viewed as a move toward reestablishing the autonomy of the university from its threatened engulfment by society, or not so good if viewed as a withdrawal from the social base upon which the university depends and to which it might contribute something positive. No one knows whether or not the cutting of these external ties has itself contributed something positive to our society.

On the whole, however, so long as students carry out their new activities responsibly, there is no measurable loss to the university. When they do not, university authorities may have to reenter and take over the function. For example, after a student sit-in in the Stony Brook library (an attempt to gain access to graduate-school research contracts), the university administration sought to have the students disciplined by bringing them to the student judiciary for occupying the university building contrary to the existing student code of behavior. The student judiciary failed to perform its appropriate function, for it held that although the offenders had acted illegally, they had acted justly for humanity in an evil world and therefore should not be punished.

But the main point is simple. All these activities are really aimed at peripheral causes rather than at any ultimate positive goals; elimination of ROTC, secret government research contracts, and war-industry recruitment, are rather loose threads actually intended as protest against our involvement in the Vietnam war. Obviously, to demonstrate against a university to obtain withdrawal from the war makes no sense. And, equally, the issues of race and poverty involve our whole society and are not susceptible to correction by demonstrations in a university. Thus, the web of involvement not only goes beyond the university but is of a character not able to yield easily to such student tactics.

We do not maintain that no demonstrations in universities have achieved redress of specific grievances. Nor do we argue that demonstrations are always useless on larger national issues. Demonstrations pointed toward specific ends—for example, passage of civil rights laws—that are restricted to nonviolent means and based on nationwide recognition of basic injustices have been successful. But demonstrations today are becoming blunt instruments, ineffective and sometimes counterproductive. And various organizers of demonstrations today think of them as merely symbolic or provocative.

But let us return to an evaluation of the objectives. Even for those who are convinced that our involvement in the Vietnam war is a serious miscalculation, there are still questions about such issues as war-related research. Can one truly distinguish between nonwar research and war research when pure physics has yielded our most potent weapon? Will our best researchers remain in universities if harassed on this issue, and if not, who will replace our top teaching talent? Is war-related research on defensive weapons legitimate in a world in which Czechoslovakias occur? And, finally, however much one agrees that peace today is essential to man's continued existence, the present university agitation against war echoes the university spirit of the thirties too closely to allow us much peace of mind.

In summary, then, however much we agree with ultimate student ideals and with the conclusion that some good has been achieved by responsible student involvement in university machinery, it is still questionable whether these ends justify the disruptive demonstrations against classes that have occurred in various places across the country. Other acts more appropriate to the ideals, more properly expressive of students' convictions, and perhaps more effective and less vulnerable to criticism might well have been sought.

IDEAL ACTIONS

Our critique of demonstrations has thus far been negative. They require such analysis, we believe, in order to tie the idealistic impulses and insights motivating the ferment to the idea of the university. Let us consider perhaps the most significant element underlying student protests: the insight into the self-generated destruction of the human species. One thing is quite clear: inchoate rage vented in demonstrations against the one institution that is most conscious of human values and of its responsibilities for their preservation is not the answer. At the same time, the answer is equally clear: trained intelligent rage can act effectively against greedy human stupidity. One of the best recent examples of this kind of action is found in the formation and subsequent activities of the Environmental Defense Fund—now centered at Stony Brook but supported by concerned scientists on a global scale. Their recent persistent court battles against the use of DDT are now finally beginning to produce significant changes in our use of this hydrocarbon which has been shown to have devastating genetic effects. The discovery and recent publication of the fact that mothers' milk today contains nearly four times the DDT allowed in cows' milk sold in California has helped to prove the necessity for banning use of this widely used insecticide.

Enraged intelligence is the source of effective idealistic action—the source that the idea of the university nourishes and that the actual processes of university life give teeth to. Such enlightened rage produces the essential human qualities necessary for success: patience, persistence, and self-sacrifice. In contrast, sporadic revolts against universities constitute mere momentary destructive vandalism. The idealist's task will not be achieved in a short foreseeable period. The student idealist must prepare himself for the most

58

effective action by becoming well-prepared intellectually, as well as emotionally, for the strenuous efforts necessary to achieve his ends.

Second, in the universities, historical and political studies of revolutions can help isolate and refine our understanding of their causes, their structures, and their effects upon society. Such study can help us seek the most effective ways to make changes that will ensure a more open and viable social structure that is responsive, without violence, to the needs of its members. Through university activity, we should be able to provide more effective means for individual citizens, including members of the university community, to act significantly in their communities to correct the injustices and defects in our society. We can then conclude that one test of the viability of a society—that is, whether or not the society should be maintained and can serve as its own means of self-improvement— might be found in the answer to the question whether the society provides the conditions for unhampered university activity.

Now the answer to the question of what contribution students can make to our problems and to the realization of their ideals becomes clearer. The special qualities they can contribute to the common human effort toward a better world are not just their idealism and their vigor but also their intelligence—intelligence trained to be effective in resolving complex problems caused by less attractive human characteristics. This is clearly the message which the Russian physicist, Sakharov, conveyed in his appeal to the American and Russian people to resolve our differences in peace. Our young idealists must be prepared to help solve problems intelligently and knowledgeably; they will not solve them by mere vigor and disruption. And the primary agency for acquiring the necessary knowledge and intellectual facility for inquiry and discovery of new solutions to our problems is the classroom, as we have defined it.

There is probably some truth in aphoristic remarks like technology has outstripped sociology, or we need a knowledge of applied ethics, or we must love our fellow men as brothers, or each man must know himself. Essential to such statements is an understanding that is not merely technical, nor morally neutral, nor emotionally sentimental, nor private to each man, but sensitively and reflexively determinate of men's problems and appropriate prospects.

THE UNIVERSITY IN HISTORY

So far we have been concerned with aims and ideals that are determined by readily identifiable ills and deficiencies. The ends have been easily identified as the positive counterpart of the negative state of affairs presently existing. But of course the means of attaining such easily identified ends are by no means obvious. The difficulties of realization do not arise merely because of complexities of the situation but also because of the very nature of human action and thought; any action can be judged good or bad, helpful or hurtful, in circumstances in which opposing and diverse estimates of the significances of the action enter. Yet thinkers have found values in human achievements that transcend the circumstances and diversities involved in immediate action. Bertrand Russell, in "A Free Man's Worship" celebrates just this transcendent power in men's understanding. In *Science and the Modern World,* Whitehead traced the place of reason in human history, especially during the past 300 years. He concluded this work as follows:

The moral of the tale is the power of reason, its decisive influence on the life of humanity. The great conquerors, from Alexander to Caesar, and from Caesar to Napoleon, influenced profoundly the lives of subsequent generations. But the total effect of this influence shrinks to insignificance, if compared to the entire transformation of human habits and human mentality produced by the long line of men of thought from Thales to the present day, men individually powerless, but ultimately the rulers of the world.[2]

Disciplined knowledge as it has developed continuously through powerless teachers and learners for 2500 years is now our best hope for the solution of present human ills, as it has been the source for the solution of many ills of the past. The center of teaching and learning is the university, and its integrity must be preserved by any

[2] A. N. Whitehead, *Science and the Modern World* (New York: The Macmillan Company, 1947), pp. 299–300.

social system that hopes to cope effectively with the ever-increasing problems of our society. What Whitehead saw so clearly was the ultimate superiority of persistent disciplined minds in effecting significant changes for mankind.

But even more important, the development of reason is also a self-sufficient value that effects changes in the way man thinks and reasons. This fact is perhaps man's best hope: even as we uncover the power to achieve self-destruction in a number of different ways, we will at the same time discover in ourselves the bases for containing these powers. Some may wonder, if Whitehead is correct in praising human reason, why we did not solve all human ills long ago. But this wonder neglects the lesson that Whitehead draws from the history of reason—that is, that man does change himself and his reason as he achieves each step and solves progressively more involved problems. Our past successes give us some hope that we may be successful in the crucial problems we now face. Again the solution depends not upon hasty and unmeditated action but on action based on clear and penetrating thinking. The continued development of this power is the precious obligation of the university.

Problems

 TWO

There are all kinds of problems in higher education today, but they have become magnified and distorted in the absence of firm principles by which they can be analyzed, evaluated, and properly disposed of. We have chosen three problems for analysis that have become prominent in the minds of the students and the public.

The first problem—the problem of curriculum determination (Chapter Five)—is central to a university. The issue centers around what questions should be raised as appropriate determiners of general university requirements. The second problem (Chapter Six) takes account of the students' beliefs that since they are the "customers" in the educational process, they should have the democratic privilege of participating in determining what is done within the university; that is, they should participate in the governance of the university. We analyze this issue in terms of what the students as consumers can indeed contribute to the running of the university. And the final problem (Chapter Seven) has been selected as illustrative of the kind of problem forced upon universities by the society in which they operate. The question is how universities can help cope with such problems.

There is no ready-made solution for the problems discussed in this part. In considering all these problems, the underlying assumption is always that the solution to the problem must be compatible with the nature of the university as developed in Part One.

Student-
Oriented
Curriculum

⚬⚬⚬ 5 ⚬⚬⚬

It is evident, so the current view asserts, that a student can genuinely learn only what is meaningful to him. This proposition is then said to be the key to judging old curricula and building new ones. Extensive curricular reform was in fact instituted during the ferment at Stony Brook on this basis. Distribution requirements prior to specialization were drastically reduced. Specialization in a major also ceased as a general requirement and became an option. Even within it the student could pursue an independent project worked out by and for himself, or he might take a broad-gauged program in the liberal arts.

These changes were considered student oriented in three respects. First, they were to give free play to the student's interests as an individual. Second, they were to enable him to deal with the "real" problems of his own life and times since these do not fit neatly into the specialized and fragmented concerns of the traditional disciplines and departments. Third, since professors in the long run depend for support on adequate student enrollment, the faculty would have to compete for students by making their courses interesting. Thus, even courses conducted under the aegis of a departmental discipline would have to adapt to the need to stimulate students and provide outlets for their creative impulses.

Student-Oriented Curriculum

The changes thus effected were presented as only the beginning. One corollary, for example, is that various activities should now be recognized as parts of the curriculum. For example, participation in university governance is considered deserving of academic credit as a course in political science; and in general, since life itself is education, the concept "curriculum" must be enlarged so that it does not fence off anyone's interest or activity. (Here is one of the points at which this topic crosses into the decline of the classroom discussed in Chapter Two.)

To appraise this "new" concept of student orientation, one must distinguish truth from principle. It is, of course, true that what a student learns must be meaningful to him. But it does not follow that student interest is the principle of a university curriculum. When we have expressed this opinion in discussions, a favorite reply is that the university exists for the sake of the students. There is no need to debate that claim at this point. Even if one takes students as the end of the curriculum, one cannot reasonably infer that student interest is the authoritative source, the principle that lays down what the curriculum's shape, method, and content are to be. The rules of reason, processes of communication, and structures of subject matter that enter into the operations of a university classroom make demands of their own.

But to argue our position in these terms gives the impression that we are against student-oriented education, which in today's climate is taken as an immediate sign of repressive reaction. However, our position is that the diverse elements that enter the classroom must be taken into account in order to understand what it is to be a student. The question is not whether the curriculum is for students but, first, who is the student it should be for? Oddly the pro-student view rarely begins with this question; in fact, the student is rarely described as a student; he is spoken of rather as a youth, or as a socially conscious person, or as an individual. What seems to make him a student is his spending his youth, or exercising his social consciousness, or giving release to his creativity, at the university. In this perspective, for the curriculum to be student-oriented is for it to be oriented to one or more of these characters.

Similarly, while there is much discussion of a life style peculiar to this age at this time in the university, there is rarely discussion of the sense in which it is a life style appropriate to a *student*. The predisposition to disparage "talk," to test truth claims by subjective reaction rather than by inquiry, to regard the teacher-student contact that centers on an intelligible subject matter rather than on personal relations as a peripheral activity—such predispositions are extreme examples of the tendency for "student orientation" to be a misnomer for orientation to the interests of those now spending their youth at the university. We here admittedly draw the picture in the extreme, but the tendency is clearly present. Let us turn then to some of the specific curriculum-reform issues raised by this approach.

DISTRIBUTION REQUIREMENTS

Before the reform, distribution requirements at Stony Brook were the remainder of the postwar push to a general interdisciplinary core of study before specialization. What is important is the grounds on which the attenuation of these requirements were argued by those both pro and con. In numerous discussions, only one question commanded attention: how many courses in what areas are needed as samples to enable the student to judge whether he is interested in the area? Those persons opposed to the reform cited examples of young people's discovering unsuspected interests for future specialization only because the generating course had been required. Those supporting the reform allowed some requirements to remain, acknowledging that student interests were not yet formed, but they preferred on the whole to trust the student's independent explorations rather than a stuffy curriculum committee's prescriptions.

What strikes us as wrong here is not the pro against the con, or the con against the pro, but the fact that *both* of them accepted the impoverished terms of the issue. Nonspecialization was conceived by both as a question of sampling for interest determinations. The traditionalists restricted themselves to the argument that the most effective sampling was by a schematized breakdown. The reformers argued for more spontaneity. As the postwar debates showed,

66

there are a number of additional important questions. How can common courses, if run well, help satisfy the critical need for bases of communication among students beginning to fragment off into specialized areas? Students immediately narrowing down to an independent study project are involved in this problem. The function of the curriculum in establishing links for communication among students is a by-product, but it can be a critical one. Of more direct concern is the value of multidisciplinary training or background to the student's subsequent work in his specialized area or independent project. There is no unambiguous measure of this value, but it involves the student's ability to see his specialized field in its cultural-philosophic context and his flexibility within the field. Finally, and more generally, the issue of distribution requirements raises the question of what constitutes an educated man in today's world. That there is and ought to be no mold does not lessen the importance in a university of each student's facing the question of what it means to be educated.

But discussion of these several issues is aborted by the use of student interest as the controlling principle, although such discussion might produce some substantive changes if university people develop a better appreciation of the purposes of the existing requirements.

EDUCATION AS EXPERIENCE AND ACTION

There is a call today for academic credit for diverse kinds of extramural activity and dormitory experiences, which is then accompanied by a call for parallel tracks of action and class work in experimental colleges. The cycle is completed with the demand that the classroom itself be experiential rather than merely intellectual. These demands are based on the "discovery" that intellect and emotions are interwoven.

The entire push here overlooks what is distinctive about being a *university* student. In teaching a child about a circle, it is well to talk of bicycle wheels and to speak of spokes rather than radii. But at some point the transition should be made to mathematics. The connection with experience is not thereby lost. Obviously, subsequent

67

"experience" of the wheel is enriched by the geometrical interval. Similarly, at a more sophisticated level, Norbert Wiener can be stimulated to the conception of mathematical problems by the motions of sea waves. The relevant mental power here is the double one of developing the capacity to think in terms of a sharply articulated subject matter, as Watson had to do in the search for the formula of the double helix, and of having the insight and imagination to be aware that the subject relates back to diverse forms of experience or action without necessarily being immersed in them. Ortega finds that man has a tendency to reflect prior to and after action. During the reflection, application to action is not erased but is suspended. This power of reflective suspension makes him distinctively human. Being a student in a university is specifically and peculiarly adapted to advance this uniquely human power. To talk about drama without having seen or acted in a play is admittedly absurd. But to criticize or otherwise reflect on plays only while in the process of staging one is equally absurd. One cannot be a university student so long as he must draw pictures of everything.

In the child's early years, one aim of education should be to keep his ideas in tandem with his acts, so that part of knowing an idea is knowing its do-ability. This early education focuses on the formation of habits. University education should be able to use that base to probe far more deeply by reflection and to focus on criteria for the success of reflective thought rather than directly on the formation of habits.

Reflective thought ultimately makes experience and action far more meaningful than they could otherwise be. Marxism transforms an underpaid worker's immediate experience of wretched circumstances into a sense of membership in a class sharing the same condition and hence on the verge of action. Lincoln's view similarly gave the condition of the slave meaning as a violation of natural law independent of any class analysis. This general point applies equally to less radical situations: the common example is that a man pounding a nail applies the same physical motion that he would use in building a home. Whether a man is only pounding a nail or is also building a home is a function of the idea that gives the same physical motion its significance. Conversely, the extent to which action and experience provide material for reflection is greatly increased by the quality of prior reflection.

Radicals like to turn the new distinction between experience and intellect to their purposes. Hence, they claim that one learns more from being hit over the head by a policeman's club than from a year in class. It can also be said that a policeman learns more from being hit by a radical's stone than from any theory. But physically the acts are the same. What one "learns" is a function of the thought that precedes and follows the collision as much as of the thud of impact.

There is a comparable dependence of emotions on the intellect. An emotion is not felt in and of itself (like pleasure or pain), but as a felt awareness of a situation, or one's relation to the world (as in anxiety). Our emotions can go no deeper into "truth" than the power of our mind to present objects for awareness.

It would be an error to focus merely on an assumed parallel between practical action and reflective thought. A university student is also capable of expanding his awareness of the kinds of whole experience that reflective thought itself can constitute; the "intellectual" need not be half an experience but a whole. The emotions attendant on the discovery and resolution of a problem intelligible only to someone grounded in the discipline are many and absorbing. Here the intellectual and emotional become reciprocal functions of each other; the emotional drives and satisfactions are required to keep the inquiry moving, to hold it together, and to provide signals of direction. Such experiences are prefigured in earlier education; a university student moves into them directly.

REAL-LIFE SUBJECT MATTER

We considered whether action must be tied to learning as concretely experiential. The coordinate question is whether the subjects dealt with in the curriculum are "real-life" problems of the times as distinct from esoteric specialties of the departmental disciplines. Students are said to be interested in the former because they are relevant. Further, the established disciplines, even at their best, deal with only an isolated part of a real problem. Air pollution, for example, or an urban renaissance, can be dealt with adequately only by a convergence of special fields.

The sharp distinction thus set up neglects the fertility of the disciplines and fails to consider appropriate attitudes of a university student toward apparently nontopical problems. Continuing research in all fields should and does yield new fields—for example, biochemistry, or the extension of economics to sociological factors, or the use of physics in engineering. Similarly, many disciplines consist to some extent of reflection on ongoing affairs. Sociology obviously draws data and laws from contemporary development; so also literary criticism cannot neglect even the new artistic pornography without defaulting on its professional obligation.

Further, the argument that special fields are necessarily limited to some narrow part of real problems is misleading. One man's whole is another man's part. Urban affairs is a whole area that involves economics, demography, political theory, and so on. Conversely, economics applies to a national and international whole of which urban affairs is a part.

In general, the issue is not *whether* special fields are applicable to life, but how. In extreme form the view that favors relevance over the disciplines would be appropriate to propaganda, as Jacques Ellul describes it. No matter how effectively propaganda works with glitteringly general slogans and with embracing ideologies, it must always, he says, keep itself tied to the timely—indeed, to the headlines in the press. Too often when someone calls on the university to emphasize "real-life" problems, the subject he cites is on the front page the day he speaks.

New subjects should be conceived on criteria of what constitutes an object of disciplined inquiry and on what achievements already have been made in a discipline. Criteria of intelligibility and coherence, for example (not simply topicality), are required to determine the researchability of a subject. Unless such criteria are applied, the subject matter may be ephemeral in the form studied, and worse, the generalizations formulated for action from the study may be needlessly dangerous. The rush to the barricades and questions of how to institute change may cause neglect of the broad bases of action. The issue in actional disciplines is not, or ought not to be, whether there should be orientation to action (if that is lacking, the discipline is false to its own field); rather the issue should be whether a university student is an object of propaganda (self-made or otherwise) or a disciplined inquirer.

We discussed in Chapter Four how a university student is especially effective in efforts devoted to the correction of social and political ills. Nonetheless, he is still in the process of making himself, and what he does now at the university will affect the shape of his moral action for the rest of his life and will lay bases for future effectiveness.

Issues of action change. A man with a broad and disciplined base can do more than respond to issues in an ad hoc, superficial way. Further, issues of action do not always come readily labeled as to their morality; a breadth of perspective and a knowledge of a range of issues in history is needed to judge them wisely. A university education offers to the student, who sees himself as such, the requisite opportunities. Such breadth does not remove one from action.

INTELLECTUAL STIMULATION

There is a massive complaint today that the curriculum is not stimulating—that it mainly transmits facts. This complaint is closely related to the call for the accreditation of experience and action in the university, but there is an advantage in considering it separately. It deals with the student more completely as a unique individual, in the ideal, whose every impulse has its value in the fact of its being his own. The real curriculum in this view is the student's own interior, the problem being its discovery, release, and development. The classroom teacher must stimulate him and maximize the occasions for self-expression. Thus, the focus moves away from moral duty (although not in opposition to it) to a life style in which excitement is a criterion of effective education.

What excites or interests one student does not interest another. The conception of an absolute standard of the "interesting" is here contradictorily combined by the proponents of pro-student reform with the emphasis on the uniqueness of every man. How can one have it both ways—classes intrinsically interesting to everyman, everyman having different interests? One of the great features of a university is the range of choice it provides, but the corollary of this range is that those interested in a subject are obligated to play their role in sustaining the interest of the class. The student should ask himself what his responsibilities are. Is it the teacher's function to discover and present what interests him on the surface, or is the student partly responsible for the viability of the classroom experience? His preparation, his participation, his reflection, and his care in appraising what the course demands of him; all affect the success of the course.

A common view is that there are but two ways of viewing a curriculum: either it is a set subject matter which the teacher dispenses on his own authority and which the student therefore receives passively, or else it is a flexible succession of topics designed to stimulate the student's individual response. But neither way marks the most characteristic process the university student does, or rather ought to, go through. The key fact in that process is that he has, or is developing, the bases for judging the adequacy of truth claims (or, in art, of "worth" claims); as we noted in Chapter Two, the exercise of this critical function depends in part on his grasping the fundamentals of a "set" subject matter. One cannot say that in this process there is a rigid line for the student between receiving a body of knowledge and responding creatively as an individual. His judgment is grounded in his own powers, although what is being judged may well be material that is "handed" to him. Thus, he does not passively receive material, but neither need he merely express himself; for his judgment should purport to be intelligible to anyone considering the problem. In such activity the student is both an individual—in the sense of being self-dependent—and he is "just like" others in seeking a reasoned agreement with them.

Such a judgmental stance, such a carrying out of a student's responsibilities, need not eliminate creativity. Creativity in the raw barely exists. The great discoveries in most disciplnes could not have been made except by those steeped in the subject matter. The road to innovation is an understanding of prior innovations and of the difficulties they lead to.

The craving for excitement now, without accommodation to the obvious features here presented, may be a condition the teacher must directly satisfy in early education; but at the university level students intent on achieving the self-dependence proper to a student know the value of laying bases now for excitement later. Facts, techniques, and principles acquired in disciplined courses now can function later in helping the student open up new lines of inquiry for himself. We do not mean to make a simple division between early drudgery and later joy. Even the laying of preliminary groundwork in a discipline should not be a deferred satisfaction. Rather, our point is that the pleasure of the early work is enhanced by the prospects of future competence implicit in it. If the early work is only drudgery, the teacher or student is at fault. Analysis, synthesis, and judgment are indispensable at every stage of learning in the university, and wherever they are present the classroom has intrinsic excitement.

But there is a peculiar irony to the situation. The more students call for more immediate stimulations, the less they are likely to provoke the kinds of changes that will make their education great. They cause the premium to be put on the flamboyant showman. But the more they develop their powers of disciplined judgment grounded in the subject matter, the more students will tend to participate so challengingly as to require a rise in the level of teaching. The most activist role for a student is being a student.

Toward a
Minimization of
Governance

⚜ 6 ⚜

Those who argue that there should be a supreme university governing body with equal or near-equal representation of students and faculty rest their case in general on participatory democracy. They also claim that such governance will bring several specific benefits. First, the student's possession of equal power will put the required pressure on the faculty and administration to engage in meaningful dialogue with students. As a result, so the argument goes, students will be motivated to think seriously about university affairs; they will develop a sense of their own worth; since the faculty will have to show them respect; and they will have the educational experience of participating in genuine dialogue. In addition to the benefits of the process of governance, it is claimed that even more substantive benefits will come from the decisions made. For example, the student voice and vote can lead to the firing of bad teachers and the hiring and retention of good ones, and the faculty would be less free to multiply ineffective teachers who publish. Finally, this body is thought of as providing the instrument through which the university at last could speak with one voice on the socio-political/economic injustices perpetrated outside the university by the nation as a whole (and indeed often with the university in a supporting role). The university would cease to be an arm of the military-industrial complex.

We could easily snipe at these arguments. For example: History shows few states so thoroughly organized to accord with the principles of radical democracy as Athens. Yet a heliastic, representative court of 501 persons, having heard both sides, voted to kill Socrates. But to cite this case is to argue by example rather than reason. No doubt one could also cite cases that point in the other direction—for example, good teachers who were fired because of failure to publish. Socrates could be cited here also, for he would have been perhaps the first to be fired by a nondemocratic university, since he refused on principle to publish. However, the issues must be considered in the context of the university's general workings.

EFFICACY OF DECISIONS

Let us consider first the worth of the decisions that come out of equal suffrage governance. One can expect better decisions with student participation because students have a direct stake in the decision and firsthand knowledge on many issues; they know better than anyone else who the excellent teachers are, and they have more to lose by their dismissal.

The plausibility of the argument tends to obscure the nature of the central question, which is, in effect, who should have what portion of the power? Assuming for the moment (unrealistically) that there is a determinable amount of power to cut up as we wish, one is likely to overpoliticize the university, to see the university as consisting of constituencies with distinct interests and claims to power rather than with top-priority academic functions. But the problem in a university is not only to distribute equitably what power there is; it is also to minimize the role of power. The essential processes of the university are nonpolitical; they favor the voice of argument over the vote. Efforts should be made to achieve ends in a way consonant with that preference for argument wherever possible. Of course, matters must often come to a vote, but often less can be decided effectively this way than is thought.

Consider, for example, a student vote on hiring and firing for the sake of better instruction. Student opinion always has been of considerable weight, in varying degrees. The proliferating teacher-evaluation surveys are now formalizing, and perhaps to a small extent increasing, this sphere of influence. If in addition students were allowed to be present at appearances of candidates for positions and were also on reappointment committees, their ability to exert influence would increase further, even if they had a voice but no vote. Their influence would increase not so much because of the prestige of committee membership but because they would be in a position to give articulate, well-defended appraisals. We feel that such reasoned evaluations should have more weight in a university than thumbs-up or thumbs-down conclusions.

Perhaps the most efficacious of all means open to students to assure a high level of teaching in the classroom is their grasp of their own responsibilities as students. If they show the attitudes and the *work* appropriate to a high level of learning, if they motivate the classroom process with questions based on study and thought and participation in class discussions, then the pressure on the faculty to do great teaching will be strong and direct. Admittedly, the effect of this pressure varies with the individual instructor; but when it is supplemented by teacher-evaluation surveys, plus reasoned student input, the classroom will come closer than it is to being the center of the educational process. Great students, not votes, have the greatest influence on the quality of teaching.

None of these devices—student evaluations and engagement—involves the vote. There are numerous issues open to similar nonpolitical methods of change. We are not arguing against the vote. We are arguing that its role in the process of determining whether there is great teaching on campus is bound to be minor.

The question of hiring and firing thus illustrates how political decision making must be put in its proper—that is, highly limited—perspective. The question of student generated curricular requirements illustrates what can happen when that perspective is not seen clearly. We take as an example the recent student-generated "reform" at Stony Brook. As we have noted, that reform is aimed at greater choice on the part of the student, toward letting him take whatever program appeals to him. No doubt the programs of individual study that emerge will be of varying value, but our concern here is to flush out the fairly obvious way the reform further extends the present tendency to politicize the university. As we have noted, the curriculum change was brought about by democratic rule. In effect, however, it does not work by majority rule, since it supports the trend toward each student having the right to choose his own plan of study. Thus, this liberty takes on a political cast, becoming a sort of academic right analogous to a civil right—the principle behind it being that the individual has a right to decide matters affecting himself. The result seems to be the insertion of the democratic cast of the new politics (in the guise of new curriculum) into a basically intellectual learning process.

Earlier we said that for us to cite the execution of Socrates by majority vote would be a sniping and unhelpful kind of argument. But it becomes relevant in our present context. The basic error of that trial was not that the Athenians misjudged Socrates, but rather that they applied a political process to an intellectual question. Socrates stayed wholly out of politics; he inquired into the nature of an ideal state, not into the relation of the tyrants of the Thirty to the democracy; he inquired not into the justice of the colonial war in Potidea, but into the nature of justice. Aligned with no party, involved in no immediate passion of the state, his was a teaching which properly should have stood or fallen on its validity as intellectual inquiry. However, the Athenians took it upon themselves to make the question of whether Socrates was right or wrong a question decidable by vote—one of history's worst examples of the politicizing of an issue proper to a university.

EQUALITY AND RESPECT

Students stress the importance of the status that power gives them. Without it they are treated as nobodies; they are not listened to. With it, they say, they have the indispensable basis for entering into dialogue with faculty and administration and satisfying their need to have functional worth. In our view, however, governance is

77

not the optimal kind of activity in which most students can find a role and status. Governance deals with the accessories, not the substance, of the processes of disciplined education. Compared with the classroom processes and the opportunity they present for self-realization, governance is a bore and a bother, although admittedly indispensable. When the crisis and novelty wear off, few remain around to mind the store.

Participation in governance does have a direct relation to study in political science and related disciplines. Even in terms of this connection the activity has to be seen as a very specialized or peculiar kind of governance without significant differences from political bodies. This may be of value, as may also just the fact of a student's feeling himself involved in affairs and thinking about education in terms of the adjustment of various pressures for change and resistances to it. But we are not here speaking to these limited objectives, but to the view of participation in governance as the means by which students assume their true role as a coordinate constituency of the university, possessed of equal power, and as a result performing their rightful functions in the rational determination of the university's life. But, as at Stony Brook, while university governance processes produce some valuable deliberations, on the whole their rhetoric provides neither the circumstances nor issues for the rational, status-giving communication which is desired.

Yet some of what the students say they want from their participation in the processes of governance lies right at hand. The respect they want requires very little outright power. Part of the effort necessary to get that respect belongs in the classroom. Here the student has the best foundation for dignity—that which Kant prescribed—he is the end for which the classroom contact occurs. Here he has the chance for a sense of worth that comes, not from mystic introspection, but from active contribution to the classroom process and from opening up new lines of thought for further development.

But why then, it is asked, have such features of the educational processes not been forthcoming? Part of the answer is that some professors fail to give the classroom its proper centrality. But

78

it is also true that in many cases classroom activities are highly eligible to contribute to the student's growth and formation of identity. The proper effect is often lost, however, because students fail to recognize the character of what is happening, or they reduce it to the anti-educational slogans ("memorization," "nonemotive," and so on) that are applicable only as rhetoric makes them so. And some students are hypersensitive to being unequal in the classroom or resent the professor's supposed authoritarianism.

In a real sense the student is not equal. To demand vote-based equality undermines part of what it means to be a student. But this status should not be determined by an antecedently fixed authority role; the teacher-student roles only set up a formal relation within which the *actual* relation emerges. Normally, in fact, the student *is* dependent, especially the student who is in active pursuit of learning. He is an equal in the sense that he is the end or purpose of the exchange; even in his dependent role, he can have formidable weight.[1]

CORPORATE SOVEREIGNTY AND INDIVIDUAL RESPONSIBILITY

As the politicizing of the university intensifies, it becomes important to question whether there should be a single body from which all rights and powers within the community flow. The proponents of the idea of a supreme governing body that is democratic give assurance that students will not usurp problems that obviously belong to experts—such as certain problems of the medical faculty. It is argued that all constituencies need not decide equally all issues; the authority to decide matters concerning qualifications of medical doctors, for example, would be delegated by the supreme body to the medical faculty, whose recommendations would be approved *pro forma*. The need is simply that there be a recognized, overarching body from which the authority stems, for that body can then act in terms of a consistent overview.

[1] A student who wants a model of how to ask a question should see the question Glaucon and Adeimantus pose to Socrates, as the supposed expert, at the beginning of Book II of the *Republic:* they put the whole of his life's work and expertise to the test by the structured incisiveness of the problem they confront him with.

The Voiceless University

We can accept such assurances but wish to challenge the concept behind it. That concept of a supreme governing body assumes that the university community is one in which there is an *indivisible sovereignty,* a single ultimate source of power. To wish that kind of sovereignty on a university is to neglect the advantages of a sprawling, loose-jointed structure as a means of keeping politics to a minimum. No one argues that a neighborhood community self-evidently has within itself a single sovereignty and must accordingly require that the activities of all the neighbors be authorized by the unicameral Neighborhood Congress. Admittedly a university is not a simple neighborhood but neither is it a political sovereign. It is a pluralism of functions, some of which center on, some of which are derivatives from, and some of which are accessory to the revitalization and advancement of knowledge. That there is a central interest in the community does not mean, however, that the functions have to be run from the same power source. The extent to which dormitory lecture-discussions are generated by or reflect some influence of the classroom is not a matter for political determination—the relation can exist without either activity's having any rights over the other.

A corollary of the single-sovereignty concept is that the overarching body can express an opinion or perform an act in the name of the university, providing that a majority so desires. Thus, whether the university wishes to issue a partisan resolution on a political issue is purely a matter for the ruling body to decide. We have heard this argued by students and faculty alike. Why not, they ask, if a majority wishes it?

Here one has a clear case of the carrying of a political rule to the point where it seriously infringes on the individual's intellectual integrity. The custom proper to a university is that men speak for themselves. Those who hold a position they wish to make public should do so as they wish, speaking for themselves. But to make their opinion a university opinion, implicating the minority, illustrates a failure to recognize that, even where a university from necessity has political institutions, they should be shaped so far as possible to bend to the nature of the university community. It is an essential part of such a community that to the greatest extent practicable, no man be committed to a position he does not wish to defend. That his "nay" vote could be on record and so reported by him does not alter the logical error of saying that in this case the majority is the voice of the university. Nothing said here argues against—indeed it encourages—collective political action and expression by those concerned, nor against publicizing one's connections with the university. In times of crisis, collective political action that is massive yet "unofficial" can carry greater weight because it is not subject to the obfuscatory charge that the university has violated its character.

ADAPTING POLITICAL PROCESSES

Suppose that in accord with our arguments we narrowed the scope of politics in the university. We still would not necessarily have bent the processes of governance sufficiently to the nature of the university. We should look for every opportunity to favor the voice of the argument over the force of the vote, and to give recognition to the fact that the university grows more by the knowledge of its members than by their felt preference.

Consider, for example, the question of qualifications of suffrage and of office. The United States lets no one under 18 vote and no one under 35 serve in the Senate. Should universities set similar qualifications in university governance? Should freshmen vote on all issues that others vote on? Should it even be theoretically possible that nontenured faculty alone "represent" the faculty in a university senate? Similarly, should universities not require that some of the students who are to be elected "Senator" or to serve on curriculum committees have satisfied higher criteria of academic achievement than admission to the university? A counterargument we have heard is that such students should instead be barred, since they will be the ones most likely to defend the status quo and hence least likely to innovate. This argument is like the claim we noted in another connection—that a physicist who has mastered ongoing physics cannot well innovate in it.

It is possible to think of groupings in the university as determined by its functions as an educational and research institution or as determined by the special interests of constituencies. We recognize, of course, that in many respects one way of looking at the groups produces about the same outcome in decisions reached as the other. But the push toward a kind of politicization of the university nonetheless blurs its difference from other institutions.

SUMMARY

We have argued that the power of the vote often cannot deliver what is sought from it, that the ends sought in the processes of governance are better sought in the classroom, and that whatever politicization is unavoidable should be shaped to the nature and functions of the university rather than to a political theory based on sovereignty and interest groups.

Of all the dangers we have noted in present trends, the most dangerous is the tendency to bring the democratic equality of the individual into the classroom as its organizing principle. This tendency has already produced the demand that within a single course the content be determined by the preference of the class, perhaps after a start provided by the instructor. How far does the principle carry? What the majority of the class decides on may not appeal to any given student. And what appeals to him today may have lost its flavor tomorrow, well before he gets a good taste of it. In the *Republic* of Plato, the virtue of democracy is that it allows each individual to do as he pleases, and this individual freedom leads toward the construction of a most pleasant mosaic. This democracy of individual men is reflected within each man; each has a multiplicity of desires, and on good democratic principles each desire is as good as another and deserves equal rights to expression and satisfaction. The policies of governance—and of nongovernance—that we have advocated deemphasize the political in order to lead away from such a democracy of desires to an intelligible ordering of those desires.

The University
in Society:
Drugs

∞ 7 ∞

We noted earlier the sense in which society only initially determines the ends of a university—its ends ultimately being self-determinative. In this chapter, we are concerned with the impact of general social problems upon the internal operations of the university. We leave to Chapter Fourteen the more general problem of the role of the university in the context of change.

There are two primary sources of general social problems: changing mores and shifts in relative status of various groups in society. *Mores* involve such factors as acceptable modes of dress, of speech, of individual behavior (pleasure-seeking); that is, matters involving individual preferences but having a public exhibition or effect. The borderline between behavior restricted by law (murder, theft, and so on) and that restricted by prevailing mores (drunkenness and pornography, for example) is not sharp. This imprecision is the source of conflicts in the courts. *Shifts in relative status* of various groups involve conflicts of interest groups (grape pickers vs. grape owners), or of religious groups, nationalities, and races who feel they have suffered from disciminatory practices of society.

Students at universities today test the boundary line between mores and law, and universities have been forced to respond practically to these issues rather than merely consider them theoretically.

The Voiceless University

In this chapter, we shall consider the universities' position on student drug use, which is clearly a case in which students are challenging society's laws. The impact of group conflict upon the internal problems of universities will be considered briefly in a final section.

LOCUS OF THE PROBLEM

Ever since institutions of higher education came into existence in ancient Greece, they have been in conflict with the communities in which they operated. The sophists were criticized as possibly subversive critics of various city-states in which they taught. Anaxagoras, a trusted adviser to Pericles, was forced to leave Athens, and Socrates was put to death by the Athenians for corrupting the youth and for not believing in the orthodox gods. Similar instances can be found through Roman, medieval, and modern times. In the thirties, Bertrand Russell, one of the world's great philosophers, was not allowed to teach at the City College of New York even though he had been granted a contract to teach logic and epistemology, because he had expressed some critical and unconventional opinions about marriage and sex. (From the perspective of current practices among many university students today, this action is clearly revealed to be ridiculous as well as oppressive.) In general, social criticism is often interpreted as subversive and consequently repressed.

In the globular thinking of some persons, police raids to enforce drug laws on campuses have constituted similar repression. In fact, at a faculty meeting at Stony Brook, one member characterized the life style of marijuana users as a threat to "the hegemony of reactionary and repressive forces" and argued that the police action was an attack upon unpopular social views and a suppression of academic freedom. However, since academic freedom is usually understood as the freedom to teach, inquire, and publish one's findings, it is difficult to establish the link between academic freedom and the right to smoke marijuana in universities.

The real issue, however, is not academic freedom of instructors to teach what they are trained and competent to teach, but unconventional behavior of students. Use of unacceptable four-letter words in the student newspapers, use of unacceptable modes of dress, and use of liquors and drugs, are typical examples of the behavior that occasions friction between the university and the community. The community views such actions as morally corrupting to the youths of the community and therefore as a danger to their stable society. Thus, the correct focus is local community relations rather than university activity.

We pass over the facts that university students are not far distant from the high school students they presumably may corrupt and that high schools had to face the problem of drug usage in towns where there are no university students to corrupt them. With the issue being fought in the high schools, it became less an issue in universities. Our focus is the character of this unconventional, illegal behavior as a type which universities must face and learn to handle with minimum disruption of their activities.

We all delight in nonstandard behavior and the imagination that it exhibits. Some have argued that such imagination is the source of new values in our culture. And perhaps this is the case in certain areas where imaginative play may add to our lives, yet we have argued elsewhere that valuable innovation requires, in addition, disciplined thought whether the novelty be in the area of science, art, or the social sciences.

What is of concern here is not the unconventional character of the action but its illegality. Hurtful actions—by students or others—such as burning buildings or injuring other persons are matters for police action. Eating goldfish, however distasteful we might believe it to be, is clearly permissible. Drug use falls between these two extremes since it does not involve direct harm to others but is illegal. This is the locus of the problem. What is the proper stance for the university in this situation?

RESPONSIBILITIES OF THE UNIVERSITIES

In the direct conflict of student drug use with laws prohibiting its sale and possession, a solution requires either changing the laws or ridding the campuses of drugs. Under present conditions, short-term prospects for either of these actions appears unlikely, although long-term prospects for both are much better. With such a situation, what are the universities' responsibilities?

We do not intend to survey the extent of this problem, which varies in intensity from coast to coast—others have done this. Nor do we intend to make fine distinctions between marijuana and hard drugs or to compare the relative effects of liquor consumption with marijuana use. The available literature argues the various degrees and levels of involvement of persons in the drug traffic and the various levels of use of drugs. Further, we do not intend to argue the question of whether marijuana leads to the use of harder and more dangerous drugs or whether marijuana as a way of life has a cumulative debilitating effect upon the user, for the biological and medical evidence is not yet clear. And finally, we are not concerned with the intensity of personal pleasure or with the socially rewarding motives drug users may have. Our concern is with the appropriate line of action for universities under the present unstable situation.

There are three major positions on the university's responsibility. Some have argued that actions that harm no one else should not become a matter of legal restraint. Others have argued that the university should not exercise police power to enforce the law because such an action is contrary to its primary educational function, which eschews the use of any force. And extremists have held that the university should offer some protection to its participants from harassment by outside law-enforcement agencies. They hold this position especially on those matters involving changing mores which may lead to changing the law about permissible behavior.

The determination to allow legally any action which harms no one else sounds simpler than it is. Should minors (whatever the age one puts on this) be allowed liquor, marijuana, or any prescription drugs? Are adults so self-contained as not to affect others when they are unable to take care of themselves? These questions merely indicate the simplistic nature of the "not-harm-others" principle. It merely indicates that legislation in this area is justifiable whether or not the particular legislation now on the books is

86

appropriate or effective. So universities cannot avoid their responsibilities on the pretext that such legislation is unwise and unnecessary.

Universities certainly cannot exercise police powers. Enforcement of laws is strictly a police matter. Any attempt by the university to police itself in this matter will inevitably sow suspicion among university personnel and harm the freedom necessary for university work. However, the closed dormitory atmosphere does contribute to the social pressure imposed on students who might otherwise avoid involvement in this illegal activity. Therefore, all university facilities must be directed toward aiding those students who wish assistance in avoiding this social pressure—for example, by finding new and more satisfactory roommates. And all university services for aiding all students should be based on a solid university position—for examples, the psychological services, dormitory supervision, advisory programs, residential organizations, and religious foundations. Thus, university authorities must support the law and the students who desire to obey the law, but they would do well to ignore marijuana on the campus, because active and effective enforcement is contrary to the structure of the university and raises more difficulties than it solves.

The university can and should offer its participants protection from harassment by outside agencies while its members pursue legitimate university activity of inquiry and of argument—of theoretical pursuit about drug use and other unconventional opinions and beliefs, even political ones contrary to those on which our country operates. Illegal activity, however, cannot be protected; the university is not a haven in which students can avoid their responsibilties as citizens.

There is today a growing body of information being provided by students who earlier were heavy drug users. Many of them now believe that that period of their lives was a waste. They felt the loss both in their role as students and in their relation to the larger total social environment. Evidently, dependence upon drugs gave them a false feeling of satisfaction, both psychologically and socially. On the contrary, the classroom activity is a shared one in which there is a cumulative meaningful experience leading to a psychologically and socially satisfying state. The sense of identity of university youth is often established in small cohesive subject-matter—oriented groups. In this process, the feeling of personal loneliness and of opposition of the young against the old evaporates as the young find their adult identities in the critical powers and substantive interests which as students they bring to maturity.

For a time, universities were caught in the middle between the students' drug use and police commissioners' drug raids on campus and state legislators' self-righteous calls to "clean up" the campus. But when the acute drug problems began to appear in the high schools, the pressure eased on university campuses. Eventually, it will no longer be an item of friction between the community and the university.

Other issues will replace this one—issues that will also arise out of the nonuniversity world but to which the university can make contributions toward a solution. One of the obvious possible issues is that of the relative status of various groups in society.

The changing place of racial minorities in this country is reflected in the universities' recognition of and efforts to carry out its responsibilities to all potential leadership elements in our society. There have been and will be attendant tension both within the university and in the relation of the university to the local community. But there is no insuperable problem; adjustments to the social needs of diverse groups present no difficulties as long as the core of university activity remains the intrinsic value sought by all students.

We have argued elsewhere that the university is not intrinsically an agency for social change. And we maintain that point now. But, in addition, when a social issue does enter into the structure of a university, it will be refined within this context as the university continues to perform its primary function. And the more zealously it does perform its primary function and claim the loyalty of its adherents to this activity, the more readily will it clarify and contribute to the social issue.

Autonomous Ideas

ᙡ THREE ᙡ

In stating the principles of a university in Part One, an autonomous idea was treated as the focal point for university activity, and simple examples were given. However, since the very nature of a university turns on this notion, it is imperative to develop it in the various areas of human intellectual interest: sciences, humanities, and social science areas. Part Three develops various aspects of autonomous ideas in these three areas: the expansion of ideas in science as illustrated by the famous Pythagorean Theorem in Euclid's *Elements* (Chapter Eight); the self-containment of ideas in the humanities as illustrated by the concept of tragedy in *King Lear* (Chapter Nine); and the reach of ideas in history as illustrated primarily by Herodotus' *Persian Wars* (Chapter Ten).

In Chapter Two, we gave diverse examples of autonomous ideas such as a self-spoofing limerick and a schema of argument. We also indicated that such ideas evolve in the pursuit of scientific problems or in the unfolding of the plot and characters within a tragedy. Further, we described the function of such ideas as the point of focus for student and teacher and as the standard by which students' and teachers' performances can be measured. And finally, we discussed the variety of such ideas—the best of which are preserved in man's best books and are available to minds prepared to study them.

This examination of autonomous ideas in these fields is intellectually central to our whole argument. We hope such exploration will evoke interest and involvement in subject matter areas. Such involvement is a beginning of the understanding that courses in higher education should elicit. These chapters may serve as tests for the educational notions we advocate, for individual responses to these ideas may confirm the validity of this notion of higher education or of this analysis of the nature of a university. However, for those interested primarily in the practical applications of our analysis, this discussion may be considered a digression from the main line of the argument. We return to practical issues in Part Four.

Science:
Expansion of
an Idea

❦ 8 ❦

We turn first to science, in particular to mathematics. We use an example from mathematics—although we could have taken examples from biology, physics, or any other science just as well—for several reasons. First, all of us have had some contact with elementary mathematics and especially with elementary geometry in the ninth or tenth grades in school. Second, the ideas in elementary geometry have a simplicity that allows simple, direct presentation and development of some nonelementary notions. Third, these ideas build most directly upon the simple deductive argument schema noted above, although this schema is applicable to all kinds of subject matter. And finally, mathematics is an integral part of most physical science today, and we can illustrate easily some of the applications of a key mathematical idea to natural phenomena, thus revealing further extensions of a simple autonomous idea in mathematics. The purpose here is not to teach science or history of science, although both shall enter here in a small way, but simply to illustrate the life within an idea as originally discovered and developed.

We have chosen the Pythagorean Theorem as our idea, for it has been known since before written records existed. The idea[1]

[1] The word *idea* is being used here in a broad way to include Euclid's

The Voiceless University

is found in Euclid's *Elements* as the forty-seventh proposition of the First Book. It reads there as follows: "In right-angled triangles the square on the side subtending the right angle is equal to the squares on the sides containing the right angle." And the forty-eighth proposition of that book is the converse: "If in a triangle the square on one of the sides be equal to the squares on the remaining two sides of the triangle, the angle contained by the remaining two sides of the triangle is right."[2] The history of this idea is vast indeed, and our account will dip into the history at various points to bring out some of the concepts bound up with or implied by this great discovery. Tied in with the history, of course, is the structure of the idea itself as this is developed in a systematic way through proofs and their developments and applications. The proofs given here will be schematic and are designed to make the meaning of the idea precise. No attempt is made to give formally complete proofs, for they are available in various histories of mathematics and in the source materials from which the histories are written.[3]

Before discussing the idea itself, we need to take a brief look at the background to its appearance in Euclid. The pre-Euclidean history of mathematics has been reconstructed by many famous historians of mathematics since the end of the nineteenth century.

Theorem as stated; that is, its specific content—the specific property of right-angled triangles in Euclidean planes and the proof structure and assumptions that give this notion its precision and validity. We are not here giving a precise logical or mathematical account and are not concerned with logical use/mention distinction or a precise determination of the boundaries of ideas, propositions, and inference structures. Later in the chapter we point to the subsequent formalization questions implicitly contained in the use of *idea*. Further, though from the point of view of twentieth-century formalization of mathematics Euclid's work is considered a study of formal relations applied to physical space, we are considering this as the "pure" mathematics, which it was in its formative period prior to Euclid.

[2] Euclid, *Elements,* trans. Sir Thomas Heath (Dover, 1956), pp. 349, 368.

[3] This exposition is based at various points on material drawn from Carl B. Boyer's *A History of Mathematics* (New York: Wiley, 1968). His book also provides further references to the subject matter for the interested reader.

Science: Expansion of an Idea

The earliest attribution of the Pythagorean Theorem to Pythagoras that we now possess occurred some five centuries after Pythagoras lived. (Pythagoras died near the end of the sixth century B.C.) The Egyptians and the Babylonians certainly knew individual cases of triangles upon the sides of which squares could be drawn so that the sum of the areas of two of the squares was equal to the area of the third square. Two special cases stand out: the triangle with sides of length 3, 4, and 5, and the triangle whose sides enclosing the right angle are equal. In this second case, the square on the side opposite the right angle is double in area the square on either side. This special case was exceptionally interesting to the Greeks, although it was known prior to the Greeks: given any square, one can draw a square exactly double the area of the original square by using the diagonal of the original square as the side of the new square.

Although Babylonian tablets contain numerous problems whose solution requires a knowledge of this proposition, pre-Greek mathematics is generally presumed to have only a limited concept of geometric proof. Therefore, this knowledge was not systematized but only crudely and partially crystallized out of space experience. Since the proposition in Euclid is found in the context of a well-developed proof structure, and since Pythagoras is reported to have sacrificed an ox in honor of one of his geometrical discoveries, it may not be inappropriate to credit him with having crystallized the idea into the general form and proof structure in which it is presented in Euclid's *Elements*. When this general form and proof structure is thus seen as bound up with a complex of mathematical ideas involving questions of experience, proof structure, and so on, it is evident that the meaning of the central idea is not given adequately in the bare formula of the theorem. Rather the meaning of the idea as autonomous is indicated by the various ideational relations involved; indeed, the set of these relations constitutes the structure and autonomy of the idea. There are five relations that make up this set—in this and most other autonomous ideas—and we will accordingly examine the Pythagorean Theorem in terms of each.

The Voiceless University

Crystallization. The first relationship has clearly been noted in Boyer—the "crystallization" of geometrical ideas (of space relations or of properties of plane figures) out of the crude matrix of experience. Clearly geometrical truths are not empirical generalizations from particular facts of perceived spatial relations, but the ideas are somehow "abstracted" from or "crystallized" out of our experience. "All triangles are three-sided" is not an empirical truth but is derived from the definition of *triangle.* A. N. Whitehead excellently describes the way in which mathematics develops progressively more abstract concepts and patterns from the regularities of everyday experience.[4] He begins with man's gradual recognition of the cyclical regularities of life (night-day, the seasons, and so on) and of the similarities of various entities. From these basic perceptions, man goes on to grasp the similarities of groups of different kinds of things (for example, the "fiveness" of five fishes and five days), and finally he develops the more abstract devices of using letters to stand for numbers of various kinds, and so on. In other places, Whitehead suggests a similar kind of derivation of points, lines, and planes from our experiences of corners, edges, and flat surfaces of solids. But the important point here is that the ideas, although derived from our experiences, largely get their significance and value from the structure of relations that also emerge from experience in this abstracting process. At this point, the mode of discovery of an autonomous idea (its crystallization) must be distinguished from the exhibition of the structure discovered. The discovery of a property of a right-angled triangle, for example, represents a grasp of the basic idea with the connections built into it—that is, in this case, that the squares on the sides containing the right angle are equal to the square on the hypotenuse is recognized along with the subsidiary ideas (assumptions) showing that this is the case. The exhibition of the structure of the idea is its proof. The

[4] Alfred North Whitehead, "Mathematics as an Element in the History of Thought," in *Science and the Modern World* (New York: The Macmillan Co., 1947).

94

proof, of course, can be found in any elementary geometry text and is given here (Figure 1a) briefly for those who may have forgotten it.

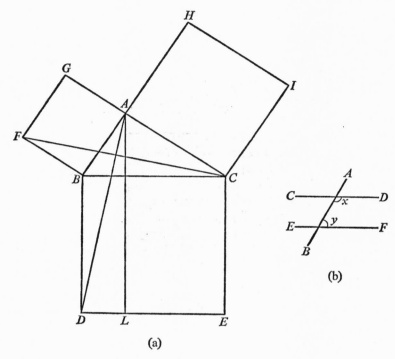

(a)

(b)

FIGURE 1

Given a triangle ABC with the right angle at A, Euclid uses three primary concepts to prove the basic proposition. First, Euclid used a previously proved proposition to justify his constructing a square upon each of the sides of the right triangle and to justify drawing a line from point A parallel to the side of the square drawn on the hypotenuse—that is, AL is parallel to BD. He argues that the angle CAG is a straight angle because it is the sum of two right angles. Second, he draws the straight lines FC and AD to form two triangles, FBC and ABD. Again he uses a previously proved proposi-

tion to show that these two triangles are congruent. They are congruent because the two sides FB *and* AB *are equal and* BC *and* BD *are equal, and the angle, included between these corresponding sides are equal, because each is composed of a right angle added to the same angle* ABC, *and equals added to equals are equal. Third, since the square* GB *and the triangle* FBC *both fall within the same parallels* FB *and* GC, *and since similarly the parallelogram* BL *and the triangle* ABD *fall within the same parallels* BD *and* AL, *he uses a previously proved proposition (that a parallelogram drawn on the same base as a triangle and within the same parallels is double the triangle in area) to prove that the square* GB *is double the triangle* FBC *and the parallelogram* BL *is double the triangle* ABD *and that therefore the square* GB *is equal to the rectangle* BL. *The same method is used to prove that the square* HC *is equal to the rectangle* CL *by drawing the lines* AE *and* IB. *And adding equals to equals, the sum of the two squares is equal to the sum of the two rectangles that make up the square on the hypotenuse.*

Now this brief and incomplete proof when fully developed constitutes the *justification* of the autonomous idea. Such a justification consists of an argument from basic assumptions to the proposition proved. The basic assumptions and the argument or proof are the second and third in the set of five relations constituting the structure of the idea. The consequences that follow from our basic idea are the fourth relation. And, finally, the fifth relation is found in the applications of the autonomous idea to the reordering of our experience.

Basic Assumptions. The basic assumptions are all the subsidiary ideas necessary to prove or demonstrate a proposition or theorem. Thus, it can be said that a proved proposition contains the totality of ideas used to prove it. In order for a proof to be complete, Euclid states as his assumptions three kinds of propositions: definition of terms, postulates, and axioms. The *terms* identify the elements of the subject matter: points, straight lines, angles, and planes. These elements of subject matter are crystallizations of our commonsense notions drawn from experience; they make it

96

possible to go from the imprecise notions of common sense to more precise and simpler notions considered apart from experience (although the content of the definitions does not play a role in the formal development of the idea). The *postulates* state precisely and abstractly the relevant properties of figures and their constructibility. One such postulate is that between any two points, a straight line can be drawn; or take the familiar Parallel Postulate illustrated in Figure 1b: if one straight line (*AB*) falls on two other straight lines (*CD* and *EF*) so that the two inside angles (*x* and *y*) on one side of the given line (*AB*) are less than two right angles, the two straight lines (*CD* and *EF*) will meet at a point on that same side of the given line (*AB*). The *axioms* state the common notions applicable to basic quantitative relations about objects (not restricted to spatial objects) greater than, equal to, or less than other objects; for example, a whole is greater than its parts, or two objects equal to a third object are equal to each other. (Later mathematicians have questioned Euclid's distinction between *axiom* and *postulate*.) The totality of these notions form a Euclidean plane and include the possible relations of lines, points, and angles within such a plane.

We restate now an important notion; that is, that any autonomous idea in mathematics not only contains the subsidiary ideas necessary for proving it, but also has its significance *limited* by the subsidiary ideas bound up with it. Thus, the idea is not and cannot be separated from the structure and limits placed on it by the subsidiary ideas. For example, the limits to the generality of the Pythagorean Theorem rest in the fact that there are geometries in which this proposition is not true. Such geometries are described as non-Euclidean and were discovered by mathematicians who replaced Euclid's Parallel Postulate by other postulates about parallels. Such discoveries indicate the possibilities of the exercise of reason in exploring truths presumably abstracted from experience; thus, any such abstraction may not be a unique reflection of what experience offers.

Further, even Euclid's conception of his basic assumptions has come under close scrutiny. For example, since the development of calculus, some mathematicians have pointed out that Euclid assumes the continuity of lines he constructs—that is, that lines do not "skip over" points—without ever mentioning this assumption.

Proof. A proof is the structure of argument from basic propositions assumed to the proved proposition. Even within the context of the Euclidean assumptions, there is more than a single route from the assumptions to a given basic idea. For example, historians of mathematics surmise that Pythagoras may have proved his theorem using arguments based on the notion of proportions—a notion that does not appear in Euclid until Book V. And looking beyond ancient Greek mathematics, we find many alternative routes for reexpressing the basic Pythagorean Theorem in structures of ideas that introduce new perspectives on geometrical relationships. For example, the trigonometric equality $\sin^2 x + \cos^2 x = 1$ is a restatement of the Pythagorean Theorem in which different relations (as compared with Euclid's work) of sides and angles of triangles are found. Or again, the introduction of the Cartesian coordinate system onto the Euclidean plane (making possible the determination of the distance between any two points in terms of the square root of the sum of the squares of the differences between the ordinates and abscissas of the two points) introduces an entirely different set of relations between lines and angles in the context of analytic geometry, in which the most general possible analysis of all conic figures is expressed in terms of a general quadratic (second-degree) equation. These two examples only indicate the possibilities for the expansion of the original idea. Each proof construction introduces different sets of subsidiary relations and the proposition so proved takes on added and slightly different significance; however, each proof reinforces the others, and the autonomous idea becomes enriched as a core notion that combines subsidiary ideas from diverse sources. This overlapping of proofs is a common characteristic of mathematical thought and contributes to the strength and recognized coherence of the whole body of mathematical knowledge.

Consequences. Fourth, we turn to certain effects or consequences of this truth. Probably around the end of the fifth century B.C., not much later than a century after Pythagoras made his great discovery, the Greeks made a very simple discovery that has had momentous importance for all subsequent mathematics. It was a discovery that grew directly out of the Pythagorean Theorem. When the Greeks noted that if one is given a square and one seeks to construct another square twice the area of the given square, one must draw the double-area square on the diagonal (hypotenuse) of the original square, they also asked the obvious question—how long is that line, the diagonal, compared with the side of the original square? They determined that there was indeed no unit of measure by means of which they could measure both the side of the original square and the length of the diagonal. They simply proved that the two lines were incommensurable—that is, incapable of being measured by a common unit of measure. Perhaps an image will make it clear how stupendous this discovery was. The outermost planet in our solar system is Pluto. Its average distance from the sun is about 3,840,000,000 miles. If we supposed that two planets were spotted just this distance from the sun but in such a way that lines drawn from each to the sun formed a right angle at the center of the sun, we would also have to admit that the straight line between the two planets could not be measured evenly (that is without remainder) by any unit of length that also measured the distance of 3,840,000,-000 miles—no matter how small a unit we might choose.

Let us describe this discovery in another way. What the Greeks discovered geometrically about lengths of lines led them to make a distinction between those which have a common measure and those which do not. Today, we express this arithmetically by distinguishing rational from irrational numbers. Rational numbers are those numbers that can be expressed as the quotients of whole numbers; for example 3/7, 17/5, 2/1,000,875, and so on. It is not hard to see that, given any two different rational numbers, no matter how close together they may be, there are *infinitely many* rational numbers between the two; for example, between 1/2 and 1/3 we can find 5/12, 9/24, 11/24, and so on. And yet, as the Greeks discovered, not all possible length relations can be specified arithmetically in terms of fractions (rational numbers). This discovery led to an historical expansion of the notion of number. The square root of 2, which is the length of the diagonal of a square whose side is 1, is not a rational number, although it can be approximated arbitrarily closely by rational numbers. The proof found in antiquity for this astounding discovery is simple. It applies the Pythagorean Theorem to a right-angled triangle whose sides containing the right angle are equal and are taken as a unit of length. Then the square on the hypotenuse is equal to 1^2 plus 1^2, which, as we know, is identical to 2. The hypotenuse is a side of a square whose area is 2, so we should say that the length of the side of that square must be the square root of 2, which we know is not rational —that is, it is not a fractional number. And this indeed is what the Greeks proved. In other words, they showed that there was no fraction that when multiplied by itself would equal two.

The proof is as follows:

Let us assume that the number identified by the name the square root of two *is a fraction and that the fraction is reduced to its lowest terms—that is, that if there is a factor common to both numerator and denominator, it will be eliminated. For example, 6/9 is reducible to 2/3 by dividing the numerator and denominator by the factor 3. Now we express this rational number reduced to the lowest terms as a ratio of two integers* a *and* b *and say that the square on the hypotenuse is equal to 2 units of area; so we can say* $(a/b)^2 = 2$ *or* $a^2/b^2 = 2$, *and we can multiply through by* b^2 *to give* $a^2 = 2b^2$. *Now we know that* $2b^2$ *is an even number, because one of its factors is the number 2. So* a^2 *must be an even number since it is equal to an even number,* $2b^2$. *This means that one of the factors in* a *is the number 2, and since every factor is squared, this means that* a *can be reexpressed as 2 multiplied by some other factor, which we will call* c. *And, therefore,* a^2 *must equal* 2^2c^2, *and* 2^2c^2 *must equal* $2b^2$. *From this last equation, we can eliminate the common factor 2 from both sides to give* $2c^2 = b^2$. *And now by a simple repetition of the argument just given—that is, that the left side of the equation is even and therefore the right side must also be even—we can show that* b *contains 2 as a factor also. Yet we assumed at the beginning that* a *and* b *had been reduced to the simplest terms—that is, that*

Science: Expansion of an Idea

they had no common factor. And now both of them have been shown to contain the factor 2. Therefore, since the argument was sound, our original assumption that the length of the hypotenuse could be expressed as a fraction must be false. And therefore there is no fraction, however small, that can be used to measure both the original side and the hypotenuse.

Historians of mathematics have noted that the Greeks inherited Babylonian mathematics, which came to them in rudimentary algebraic form, but that in making this discovery, the Greeks were led to restate all mathematics—even number theory—in geometrical form. Much later, mathematicians developed a symbolism and a method for restating geometry in algebraic terms. Descartes, in the seventeenth century, introduced the notion now known as the Cartesian coordinate system applicable to the Euclidean plane, thus initiating this development.

Yet mathematicians recognized in the discovery of incommensurable lines a great problem that reappeared in different form in the nineteenth century. They asked the now obvious question: if there is no common unit of measure for the side and diagonal of a square, how can we order in some serial fashion various incommensurable lengths? And Eudoxus, probably the greatest mathematician of the pre-Euclidean period, solved this problem by introducing a new conception of proportion, or the equality of two ratios of magnitudes. About 2200 years later, Dedekind, a great nineteenth century mathematician, resolved this problem in an entirely different context by showing that irrational numbers could be defined as a cut—that is, a special class of rationals, all members of which are either less than or greater than the irrational the cut specifies. He thus achieved in arithmetic terms what Eudoxus solved in geometric terms.

Applications. Fifth and finally, the Pythagorean Theorem has been used in physics in many different ways. It has been used to express distances in terms of right-angled factors on a coordinate system. But further, physical descriptions of the forces acting on bodies is many times given by considering the forces as combinations of component parts at right angles to each other. And the relations of the component parts or forces to the combination of the components (the original path or force) is expressed by the relation stated in the Pythagorean Theorem: the sum of the squares of the two component forces is equivalent to the square of the original force. For example, the motion of planets around the sun or satellites around the earth is conceived as a composition of two primary factors: the component due to inertia—that is, the law that a body will move in a straight line at a constant speed if no force is acting upon it—and the component due to the gravitational force that, if the inertia component were absent, would bring the satellite with constant acceleration (and increasing velocity) toward the center of the object around which it was previously moving. The first component without the second would yield a path like a tangent to a curved path (the orbit) and the second without the first would yield a line from the curved path to the center of the curve—that is, a line perpendicular to the tangent line. Thus, the balance of these two right-angled forces describes in terms of Newtonian physics the stable path or orbit of satellites around central bodies of large mass.

Or again, a similar use is made of this right-angled relationship when two subatomic particles (called "alpha particles") moving at right angles to each other collide. The resultant momentum of the collision is the square root of the sum of the squares of the momentum of the two particles prior to the collision.

CONTINUITY IN INNOVATION

The preceding account of mathematical achievements initiated by the discovery of the Pythagorean Theorem reflects the strong contrast between early and modern mathematics—particularly the contrast between the relatively elementary spatial abstractions of Greek geometry and the increasingly abstract or formal nature of modern mathematics with its nearly unlimited generality. Nonetheless there is a perceptible continuity from the original idea. The account we have given of the Pythagorean Theorem as proved within Euclidean geometry contains the seeds of the primary ideas out of which the greater abstractions and formality of contemporary mathematics has developed.

What crystallized in Euclidean geometry besides the particular relations of the concepts developed was the notion of a proof as built upon the basic assumptions of the system. More particularly, the basic assumptions, the proofs, and the proved propositions constitute what contemporary terminology would call an *axiomatic system*. In modern mathematics, increasing attention has been focused on the notion of an axiomatic system.[5] Much discussion has been generated by Euclid's distinction between axioms and postulates. Twentieth-century mathematicians have essentially discarded this distinction and at the same time have built their axiomatic systems on only one kind of sentence: axioms with undefined primitive terms. No explicit definitions are needed; the meanings of the undefined terms emerge in the relations established in the theorems proved from the axioms.

The evolution of the notion of an axiomatic system has developed from a concern for the formal structure of the system itself, and this formal concern developed in large measure from an interest in the content of Euclid's basic assumptions—in particular, the famous Parallel Postulate stated above, which is used in the proof of the Pythagorean Theorem at the point where the notion of a parallelogram is introduced. This postulate appeared less intuitively acceptable than the other basic assumptions, and various geometers attempted to show that it could be derived from the other assumptions and thus that it was not an independent statement. They failed, however. Eventually an Italian geometer attempted to show that the postulate was not independent by assuming that the postulate was false and attempting to deduce a contradiction from a postulate contrary to Euclid's Parallel Postulate taken jointly with

---

[5] See Raymond L. Wilder, *The Foundations of Mathematics* (New York: John Wiley, 1956), especially Chapters I and II, and Howard Eves and Carroll V. Newsom, *An Introduction to the Foundations and Fundamental Concepts of Mathematics* (New York: Rinehart & Co., 1958), especially Chapters I, IV, and IX.

the other Euclidean assumptions. The reader will note that this is the method of indirect proof used to show that the square root of two was not a rational number, in which case a contradiction was generated from the assumption that it was a rational number. In this case, no such contradiction was generated. And since that time, other geometries with diverse assumptions about parallel lines have been developed and found to be just as valid or consistent as Euclidean geometry; that is, no contradiction is derived from the premises.

This development of non-Euclidean geometries forced the recognition that Euclidean geometry cannot be assumed to describe physical space (a notion apparently held by some thinkers) and led to the belief that a core of mathematical problems is bound up in the examination of various possible axiomatic systems with diverse assumptions. Such axiomatic systems are investigated to determine whether or not they are consistent, whether the axioms are independent, and whether or not the system is complete, in various technical senses of these terms.

These developments raise questions not merely about diverse possible geometries but about the very form or structure of all mathematics. It is interesting to note in passing that during the seventeenth century, Hobbes and others argued that Euclid's postulates and axioms were merely disguised definitions and that geometry is based simply upon definitions of terms. But this is a different chapter in the notion of an axiom system. Our point here is simply that the form or structure of Euclid's *Elements* is also bound up within the autonomous idea proved in the conclusion of his first book.

Thus, mathematics builds upon its past achievements even as they have sometimes changed directions and emphases. Its history could hardly be conceived as merely a succession of different and mutually exclusive theorems, as has been argued in the case of the physical sciences. There are philosophical questions about the nature of the mathematical enterprise, which are evident from the diverse ways the mathematical subject matter and structure have been construed. It is even more obvious that questions about the status of mathematical objects introduce fundamental philosophical questions.

It is pertinent to note the present importance of such philosophical considerations, since they are bound up with the evolution of mathematical thought we have sketched, and since they provide a further measure of the push of the original idea in the minds of men. The precisely related ideas involved in the network of mathematical concepts indicate the public and objective nature of this knowledge as this constitutes parts of the minds of the individuals who participate in or contribute to the ongoing development of this knowledge.

Humanities:
Self-Containment
of an Idea

9

While we have illustrated the autonomy of an idea in geometry and science, it is important that our argument be seen as applicable to a full range of disciplines. Hence we turn next to an idea rooted in the humanities—the concept of tragedy.

Of course *tragedy* is less precise than *triangle* and is subject to more variable treatment. But the concept of tragedy can nonetheless have a precision suited to its function and end (just as a photographer's instruction to "stand just there" is not precise to the millimeter but is definite enough). Although many plays regarded as tragedies differ radically from each other, this variation does not mean that the concept of tragedy is not autonomous. The varied treatments of it can constitute a range of possibilities within the idea rather than give evidence of its vagueness.

One means of giving a brief indication of the autonomy of the idea of tragedy is to look at its derivation from experience. We are not here considering how tragic dramas evolved from less complex art forms and religious festivals, but rather how the idea of tragedy embodied in those dramas draws on life outside the theater. Whereas the geometrical objects of the Pythagorean Theorem were

106

Humanities: Self-Containment of an Idea

also derived from experience—by abstracting breadthless mathematical lines and triangles from the concrete and physical features of "real" lines and triangular shapes—the idea of tragedy is derived from real experience in a very different way. Life presents events that we call tragic—such as the sudden collapse of a building—but the idea of tragedy is not developed by refining or formalizing such an event into an intellectual entity as in mathematics. Rather one tends to fill out (rather than thin out) the real event to the point where a complex of features are bound together. For example, if, after we respond to an accidental death as tragic we are told that the man who was killed was a Hitler on his way to order a mass execution, we amend our view. We begin to fill out the notion of tragedy with the requirement that the person be of a certain moral worth. Or if the death came to a good man instantaneously, without advance warning, we consider whether the idea of tragedy must include suffering. There is also the question of philosophic or symbolic meaning in the event. From such a filling out, a (not "the") concept of tragedy may emerge that takes into account a full range of features we think we must know about before we can feel something is truly tragic. It is then an autonomous idea because it has all the elements, such as nobility, suffering, meaning, and so on, necessary and sufficient to make a homogeneous whole of a specified kind.

Sensitive critics often see two uses of the term *tragic,* one colloquial and one more purely spiritual. This spiritual quality is thought to lie outside the ken of ordinary men or at least outside their ordinary responses. But the critics who elevate the spiritual in literary tragedy to this rarefied height are open to the charge that they are separating art from life. As we have noted, the abstractive process from experience to the idea of tragedy is of a special humanistic kind—it consists in making the fragmentary and corrigible reactions of "life" into mutually reinforcing elements of an integral experience. Thus, the humanistic concept does go beyond ordinary life and language, but it does so by reorganizing them rather than by transcending them.

107

The Voiceless University

In treating a geometrical idea we indicated the assumptions it rested on and the logical methods by which proofs of it were developed. Again, tragedy is involved in these same features of autonomy, but quite distinctively. The assumptions involved— such as the kinds of probabilities operative in a particular work— must be posited in that particular work. For example, throughout *Hamlet* there is providence in the fall of a sparrow, but in much of *King Lear* men are to the gods as flies to wanton boys. Similarly, the "proof" in tragedy is the drama itself, and artist and audience are predominantly interested in this concrete embodiment rather than the abstracted concept.

Accordingly, it will be fruitful here to focus on a single tragic work. Of course a great work cannot be confined to any one idea, no matter how complex. The multiplicity and diversity of interpretations are evidence of an inexhaustibility which no overview could encompass, especially in the light of the cultural and intellectual contexts which add to its meaning. Yet a given experience of a drama or a given interpretation of it necessarily deals with a finite selection of features and meanings, even though they carry distant resonances with them; and when the experience is both absorbing and discriminating, this means more with regard to autonomy than that it hangs together. "I like Ike" hangs together but normally only as a fragmentary experience. In an absorbing experience of a great play, including the discrimination and grasp of meanings given by selected features of its cultural context, the play constitutes a self-sufficient world of thought, action, and feeling. The reason the spectator does not rise from his seat to interfere with events on stage is sometimes simply that he knows the rules of the game for an audience, but sometimes it is rather that the world of the play as he now perceives it is so complete that he is not aware of himself. A play so perceived is a paradigm of the autonomy we will illustrate here. Our purpose is not to argue one interpretation against others— a great play supports an indefinite number of them—but to develop one of the best of them in enough fullness to show how an idea can achieve in the concrete the integrity and independence modelled in the humanities. For this purpose we have chosen *King Lear*—in particular an interpretation of it which shows the play providing a total experience as a tragedy.

Aside from our dependence on the reader's familiarity with the play, we are using *King Lear* as illustration because it develops on its own rather than in conformity with the usual formula. Normally, the tragic hero is at the center of action; he possesses power or is in some way a definite agent. *King Lear* opens with the protagonist giving up all power, and he remains the patient in that sense until the end, dependent on others even for his "pension." Where normally the tragic action consists of the protagonist's fall from eminence, Lear's fortune is made to appear as low as it can go by the middle of the play. Normally, we first meet a tragic protagonist as a sympathetic, perhaps admirable man in his prime. We meet Lear as an old man, at the edge of dotage, vain, foolish, and tempestuous. In short *King Lear* is a tragedy in a class by itself, yet it is also rightly regarded as one of the greatest representatives of its genre.

A necessary condition of an autonomous idea is that there be criteria of its completeness; in a tragedy, such criteria at least begin to be set up at the opening of the play. We first see Oedipus as the leader to whom the people look to save them, and this status is a measure against which we gauge his fall later. But *King Lear* does not open thus. Rather it begins with a complex tragedy— a quick and specious one, to be sure, but nonetheless a total tragedy in mock miniature. The opening scene unfolds its high expectation (that the daughters will show their love to the aged Lear and that he will retire to Cordelia to set his rest on her "kind nursery"); the reversal (Cordelia will not publicly profess her love); the discovery (that she therefore does not love him); the tragic outcome (Cordelia is banished and disowned, and Lear suffers her loss—"so be my peace my grave" *I, i*)—but it does not ring true. He next appears returning from a hunt and calling out that he is not to wait "a jot" for dinner.

The play also ends with his losing Cordelia. The final scene unfolds its high expectation (that Edmund's death sentence against Lear and Cordelia will be forestalled, leaving Lear with the one thing he now wants: to be with Cordelia—"He that parts us shall bring a brand from heaven" *V, iii*); the reversal (Lear and others fail to save her); the "discovery" (her breath will not mist the stone); and the tragic outcome (Cordelia lost—"Thou'lt come no more" *V, iii*). Lear cracks and dies.

What was specious in the opening is authentic at the close. Initially he says he will "unburthened" crawl toward death, as he insists on his hundred knights and the name and additions of a king. Thinking to relieve himself of the cares of power, he yet warns Kent not to come between the dragon and his wrath. At the close, on the other hand, before Cordelia's death, the need for authority is gone and he can call out, "Let's away to prison" (*V, iii*). Again, initially he can accept her loss although she still lives. At the close, however, he cannot accept it, although as he says, he knows she's dead as earth, and he dies "pretending" to see her lips move. Her worth is such that all who do not lament her as he does are to him but "men of stone." The play thus has moved from a father's spurious experience to his authentic experience of the loss of a daughter, an unparalleled woman, under circumstances that maximize his loss. The close is an ending not simply because the plot lines are played out but more precisely because the beginning has been reversed.

The beginning thus has set up an initial measure for the completeness of the play. We do not claim that the play satisfies some generally accepted criterion of unity but that the play to a significant extent sets up the criterion itself. That is, the concept of unity as well as the concrete unity is generated by the play. This boot-strap power of art is a notable, often neglected, feature of the autonomy of an idea.

We have dealt only with a part of the self-generated criterion of unity, as set by the opening scene. The criterion is filled out in the process of change that Lear undergoes, a process that fits the tragic frame set by the opening. Why does the tragic unity of the play require that Lear change so radically? He is more fixed of character than Oedipus, yet Oedipus changes less. Why?

Humanities: Self-Containment of an Idea

One answer is that at the beginning of *Oedipus Rex,* Oedipus knows that it would be incredibly tragic to be discovered a parricide and an incestuous husband. All he does not know is that the terrible facts apply to him. But the beginning of *Lear* makes a point of showing us that Lear lacks the character and perception to understand how tragic it could be to lose Cordelia. He would not know the meaning of the terrible fact. To bring Oedipus to his tragic outcome, it is necessary only to reveal his past to him; to bring Lear to his, it is necessary to change his power of judgment and appreciation.[1] Thus, the criterion of completeness we have noted in the opening carries into Lear's change as a gauge of its relevance to the tragic unity.

We have then a lead-in or a formal condition of the play as autonomous. Our purpose is not literary criticism, but since in this case we are seeking to illustrate aspects of autonomous ideas by examining a self-sufficient component in a longer continuity (whether of the Pythagorean Theorem or of tragedy in the large), it is useful to fill in the idea of *Lear* before fanning out into the larger context of the idea of tragedy. This filling-in can be achieved by exploring the dominant element in the tragedy of the play—an element which grows out of the concrete focus on Cordelia's loss, the movement of the work, and the "world" of the play.

TRAGEDY OF SUFFERING

To generalize the focus of *Lear* into a specific concept raises the question of the assumptions from which it is developed. We could technically posit such elements as action, style, and character, and such postulates as the constructibility of these elements into serious, surprising, or other dramatic qualities, but this course would get us into a choice of available modes of criticism at a level not appropriate here. Rather we assume that various species of tragedy exist[2] and that *Lear* is an exemplary case of one of them—the trag-

---

[1] Norman Maclean, "Episode, Scene, Speech, and Word: The Madness of Lear," in R. S. Crane, *Critics and Criticism* (Chicago: University of Chicago Press, 1952), p. 601.

[2] Aristotle, *Poetics,* 1455b.

111

edy of suffering. Whatever the critics disagree on, they yet agree on the unusual intensity and extent of suffering in the play. In making that fact the basis of a species of tragedy we will thus be developing the structure of the play that must be presupposed in partisan critical disputes.

The formal context we noted earlier makes the process of suffering central; Cordelia's loss at the beginning sets the focus on Lear's anguished reaction, and this focus is sustained throughout the play as Lear in turn undergoes mistreatment by Goneril, Regan, the storm, and so on, these being parallelel by Gloucester's and Edgar's suffering at the hands of Edmund. The parallel is so sharp and so focused on suffering that Edgar can take consolation from seeing "our betters bearing our woes" (*III, vi*). Storm drenchings, eye gouging, cliff jumping, metaphorical descents into pits of hell— these are but stages to the end. And that end is presented as such that heaven's vault should crack, bringing Lear's "fortunes" far below what had appeared to be their bottom in the middle of the play.

Since it is not common for the tragedy of suffering to be set up as a separate species from other types, let us make some explanatory observations here. Few tragedies center on suffering, but *Lear* opens with it and never lets go. Even Lear's age fits him for it; for a man in his prime to be so knocked about by daughters and dukes would take away his stature, but a Lear can preserve it, not only because the old fire is still in him but also because his age does not require the exercise of counterforce. As he so often says, it is patience he needs; he is not supposed to be an agent at eighty-odd. Other tragedies focus on factors leading up to the suffering or on the affirmations or the purifications of character that transcend it. The dénouement of *Oedipus Rex* is nearly all suffering, but the main action is not. It is rather a search and is fearful not because it is painful but rather because it is so clearly leading to the painful.

As for the regeneration-in-tragedy theme, Lear undergoes a purification of character. But the purification is not sufficient to

112

enable him to surmount or even to accept Cordelia's loss (whereas in Job's case, his illumination at the end causes him to accept all) nor does it bring him the slightest solace.[3] Indeed, Lear's character is not what is noted by the survivors at his death. In other Shakespearean tragedy the survivors do focus us on whatever nobility or greatness of soul the protagonist has shown: Brutus dead is honored by Antony; Antony by Octavius; Coriolanus by Aufidius; Othello by Cassio; Hamlet by Fortinbras. For Lear there is no such word. One may object that Macbeth is blamed, but that is the point; Lear is neither praised nor blamed. Rather, what is said of him in the closing lines bears wholly on his suffering: that he is in "great decay" (Albany); that he has been too long stretched on "the rack of this rough world" (Kent); and, in summary of the play, that Lear "hath borne most" (Edgar) (*V, iii*). The tragic fact is that his progressive ennoblement of character makes him progressively more capable of perceiving the nature of his final loss when it comes. Dramatically, his partial regeneration is for the sake of his suffering. At one point, Edgar judges his situation to be the worst possible; a moment later he sees the blinded Gloucester and moralizes that it is not the worst so long as we can say it is the worst (*IV, i*). The idea of *King Lear* is that in this world of "general woe" (*V, iii*) the loss of a Cordelia and her love is by far the worst, and Lear is the only man with the bonds and the perception to grasp the sorrow. The wonder is, Kent says, that "he hath endured so long" (*V, iii*). What kills Lear—and Gloucester—is not an illness or a wound but the sheer feeling of sorrow. And since Lear has borne the most, then when he dies there is no one to say authentically that it is the worst. Thus, by Edgar's logic, in truth it now is the worst.

A calculus of pains will not take the measure of suffering in tragedy. In a play such as *Oedipus Rex*, a final lengthy scene is required for his suffering since suffering for him means the process of absorbing his fall; time is needed for him to take in (and reveal to us) its complex dimensions. In *Lear*, suffering enlarges even more

[3] W. R. Keast, "The 'New Criticism' and 'King Lear,' " *op. cit.*, pp. 134–135.

—in fact and in concept. It not only involves Lear's pain and the taking in of what is happening to him, but also includes the process he has to go through in order to be able to do the taking in. And it includes also therefore the activity of responding imaginatively at every stage in such impassioned reactions (as in his stormy speeches to the storm) that they lead to his self-reconstruction (as in the sympathy for others he discovers in the storm). More important, Lear's suffering includes his setting forth his grievances and losses with such poetic power and feeling that they finally fill the world of the play.

In most such tragic cases, the protagonist thus regenerated is plausibly expected at the close to show an improved moral sense and some reconciliation with misfortune and to acknowledge his responsibility. Lear does neither as he laments Cordelia at the close. Rather he wishes a plague on men we know to be the noblest in the play; if Cordelia is slain, all men are murderers. Further, even though he had been purged of his rage earlier, Lear's fire returns (adding at the close another echo of the opening). Without this resurgence—were he merely the purged and self-described "old and foolish" (*IV, vii*) Lear of the reunion—he would be incapable of a grief commensurate with his loss. His own responsibility, like Goneril's death (as Albany says of it), is but a trifle there.

Dostoyevsky plunges men into suffering so that they can be reborn. *King Lear* only explores its dimensions in search of a limit, itself the end. There is no rebirth, not even acceptance, but this does not mean that there is no achievement. None is more unsought, but yet none is more proper to man. At funerals we seek to experience the feelings and thoughts adequate to their object—the dead and our loss of them. The tragedy of suffering probes the conditions and nature of a sorrow adequate to the loss of exemplary human values. The values Cordelia embodied were such that for her to have lived would have redeemed all sorrows Lear had ever felt, he says; but it falls to him alone, as her father and the person who loves her most and also as the man most able to gauge her worth, to embody the sorrow. This sorrow, rather than the incomplete purification of an overly possessive old man of weak judgment, is Lear's unhappy but awesome achievement.

TRAGIC MOVEMENT

We are now in a position to test the filling out of *Lear* as the analogue in art to a proof in science. Taking the work as self-contained, we drew from the structural relation of the opening and closing the hypothesis that the work's unity lies in a reversal in what Lear suffers. This reversal we took as a lead to the species of tragedy. With the internal limits and the species of the idea now partly at hand, we can use them as the framework for examining the tragedy as a sequence—as an unfolding of its idea.

The question is how and why the play gets from the spurious opening to the close. To begin an answer, we must remember that we are not analyzing a natural situation but one presented to us as bearing signs of developments to come. The audience is expected to read the signs. That Lear is in for trouble is clear from the opening scene. The fatuousness and vanity of the ceremony he plans, together with his age and succession of rash misjudgments, suggest that he is not too fit to rule; but he is also psychologically unfit not to, for he does not know himself apart from this imperious role. When later Goneril checks him, he can only say, "This is not Lear" (*I, iv*). It is obvious that he is in for shocks and that he will respond to them on a massive—yet necessarily impotent and psychologically costly—scale. We also have some signs of the potentiality for the more perceptive and more responsive Lear who finally emerges. There is evidence of past good judgment in the fact that he had singled out Cordelia over other sisters and that he had given preference of appointment to such a forthright man as Kent and had won his loyalty; and there are evidences as well that he at least regards himself as committed to moral and human values of a high order.

Whereas in our first treatment of the opening scene we only made a formal comparison of it with the last scene, we see it now as projecting the abuses Lear will be subject to and the consequent internal upheavals in him when he is at an age and fixity of character least capable of coping with them. Signs show also that he will not be able to cope with the recognition, when it comes, of what he has done to Cordelia. Finally, the scene shows us signs of judgment and worth in him that can act as sources of self-condemnation and as seeds of change in insight. In brief, the push and potentiality for the outcome—as well as a measure for it, which we previously noted—are present in the opening. An autonomous humanistic idea can begin to unfold when it has this measure and energy for completion. It is unlike a scientific idea in that the potentialities are still necessarily obscure, some visible only to hindsight, and in that it sets up its own standards far more freely than do the premises of a scientific idea.

The unfolding occurs in a drama at several levels; we will note two of these to see how they mesh. There is in this play a level of material events—logistical change-of-place relations. The plot moves around the question of Lear's union with Cordelia. He is initially to be with her permanently but she is banished, and he goes to the sisters. As his stay with them grows more precarious, we hear that Cordelia is following events and then that she has come to Dover. When Lear is turned out into the storm, the plot turns on the effort to get him to Dover; and when he is in Dover, it turns on the effort of Cordelia's men to capture him for her—and finally Lear awakens in her tent. After this reunion, the battle lost, they go off together to prison, until separated finally by her death. It is easy but misleading to let the complexities of the play obscure the clear logistical sequence of the plot: union, separation, reunion, separation. This chain provides the skeleton for the focus we first noted, although we have not yet considered the incident it pivots on—the reunion.

At the next level are the immediate causes and issues bound up with this motion. Lear's trials and perturbations begin immediately. The slights from Goneril send him into outward rage invoking darkness and devils; and his soliloquylike statement that he had wronged Cordelia is an involuntary sign of a turbulent shame within, although it is still too early for him to adjust to his impotence: "To take't again perforce. Monster ingratitude" (*I, v*). His

116

age compounds the wounds, for he is shamed that involuntary tears should so shake his manhood.

Convulsive and curse-provoking as the rage and suffering are at Goneril's, they nonetheless derive somewhat from incredulity that this should be done to him, and in his indignation he can feel that he still has a daughter left to fall back on. But these props to dignity disappear at Regan's, and he must encounter the superior stance of the fiery duke, Kent in the stocks, and Regan outdoing Goneril. These indignities not only deepen the wounds but also call into play new modes of reaction touched with a note of desperation that sometimes inflames Lear's responses but also sometimes makes him try to repress them ("I'll forbear" *II, iv*). Even when Lear praises Regan's virtuous attitude toward her father ("thou shalt never have my curse" *II, iv*), the speech reflects a desperation not present at Goneril's and perhaps never before present in his responses. Instead of being hypersensitive to indignity, as with Goneril, he forces himself not to hear Regan's disrespect; his praise of her for knowing her duty is worded as if he is trying to make it true by saying it is. The physiological experience keeps pace as "this mother swells up toward my heart" (*II, iv*). The rapid alternations between unwonted efforts at patience and unrestrained outburst add their toll.

Yet Lear never becomes pathetic (we always have the Gloucester contrast). He does verge on the pathetic when his resources are overtaxed by the need to cope with fresh changes; for example, when at the end of Act II his daughters vie with each other in cutting the number of knights they will allow him, he is reduced to calculating their love by the size of the allowance. Yet even in this situation he still dominates. The force of his outrage, the intensity of his feelings, the quality of majesty, and particularly the rapidity and diversity of his perceptions of the situation, all culminate in a forceful defense of his need of a retinue and his refusal to endure their loss. His plea is anything but plaintive; yet it remains a form of suffering since it is an expression of outrage rather than a potent determinant of the decision.

This process is carried through in the storm, the encounter

117

with Edgar, the farmhouse trial, and Dover. Although the torment seems to have "peaked" at each point, it continues to build and to develop further variations in anguish and response until he is bound to his wheel of fire late in Act IV. His madness but measures the point at which the cuts are too deep to bear "consciously" but also are too deep not to be at the center of his thought and expression. (On seeing Edgar, he supposes Edgar's daughters have brought him to this.[4]) We will take this process for granted, then, since for our purposes it only repeats—although of course what it repeats is just the process in which his suffering becomes continually more powerful and varied, both in changes of pace and in levels of response.

But we need to note how the build-up of the suffering adds new levels and prepares for the close. For example, when the sisters vie at cutting his retinue and the question of why he needs any men at all is raised, he, for the first time, desperately discovers a philosophic defense of what he had always heretofore been able to take for granted; "O reason not the need" (*II, iv*) is such a defense and turns him to the theme of the relation of nature and value. Once set up, this philosophic theme provides a new measure of what he undergoes. "Nature" is first minimized against symbolic values; then Edgar is seen as the learned Theban because he is all nature, the unaccommodated thing itself; then nature becomes the lust and greed of all; and so on. Thus, the new level comprised of Lear's tendency to see the world as a mirror of his situation makes the content of "philosophy" itself painful. Similarly, this theme reappears as a stylistic device of, for example, using clothes to represent the symbolic values. Thus in "reason not the need" he takes what "thou gorgeous wearest" as the analogue to his retinue; at the next stage of thought, seeing Edgar in the storm, he tries to disrobe ("off, off, you lendings" *III, iv*); and in the next stage robes and furred gowns hide all, until finally in Cordelia's tent the proportion between garments and nobility is restored.

From material plot, then, through the diverse levels of experience the causes and process of his suffering deepen and diversify.

---

[4] Norman Maclean, *op. cit.,* pp. 612–615, and for the analysis of Lear's madness, pp. 600–611.

But it is all headed somewhere—to the reunion with Cordelia. This reunion is a reversal of fortune, but, more important, it is a discovery scene in which Lear learns that her filial bond still holds and that her worth exceeds whatever he could have imagined. All that precedes makes possible this perception and appreciation—again from the material to the experiential levels.

Lear's own injuries make him explicitly sensible of the injury he has done Cordelia. While it is true that he is more sinned against than sinning, a sovereign shame so elbows him that he tries to escape the reunion, even in madness. Further, he thinks he now knows her worth, but he assumes he has forfeited her affection. Finally, even awakening in a tent safe, with his great rage purged physically, he still sees himself bound upon a wheel of fire, better left in his grave; yet this self-view is what makes him capable of discovering what Cordelia is. The gentleness and respect she shows him on his awakening follow from her having empathetically focused before the waking on his earlier suffering.

Although this background leads us to expect the discovery in the confrontation scene, it still comes with unexpected force. The point is not that Cordelia greets him with the signs of formal respect ("my royal lord" *IV, vii*) or asks his benediction. Rather her appraisal of the past reveals her more clearly than before to Lear (and to us). He would not find reprisal from her unexpected, he says; at least she had some cause. And when she states that she has "no cause, no cause" (*IV, vii*), the meaning of the statement she had made in the opening scene—that she loved him according to her bond, nor more nor less—comes full circle.

Ironically, Lear's physical condition is such that after this discovery the doctor should say, "Trouble him no more" (*IV, vii*)'. To say that even pleasure causes him suffering is playing with words, but nonetheless the whole work has led to this scene, which in turn lays the basis for the monumental grief that ends the play.

WORLD OF THE PLAY

We now have the play as an articulated idea that sets and meets its own criteria of completeness and provides a unique instance of a species of tragedy. We have sought to show that these criteria apply not only to the forward motion of the work but also to its inclusion of a full range of the levels of experience in an action. We can now turn to the final peculiarity of autonomy in a complex humanistic concept. Its mode of abstraction, as we noted earlier, is not from a sensibly concrete to a nonconcrete form but from the unordered concrete to the ordered. In this sense, while the play is an abstraction from "real" life, critics can speak of the thing thus abstracted as a "world." Such an idea is infinite in that one can ask indefinitely about the relevance of particulars in that world to it as an ordered whole.

The value Lear seeks is not a practical objective, as is the revenge of Hamlet or the recovery of honor of Coriolanus, but rather "rest," "comfort," "peace" (*I, i*)—in brief, surcease at first from the cares of the throne and later from the agitations of his situation. He needs what Aristotle calls a happy old age—one that comes on gradually and without pain. Just as the end sought and denied is peculiarly appropriate to this species of tragedy, so is the basic deficiency in Lear's character appropriate. (Of course his "flaw" in judgment occurs in the initial scene. But we raise now the question of his makeup at this stage of life.) Comparison of the old Lear with the young Hamlet is revealing. Hamlet needs to act, and his tragic difficulty is that he lacks a principle of action; Lear needs rest, and his tragic difficulty is that he lacks a principle of internal peace. All his traits conspire against him. He has an inveterate tendency to rich and sweeping surges of feeling. There is no mellowness in the old man; he is mercurial and endlessly imaginative in projecting his situation. His mode of relating to others is also a root of trouble. He combines an inestimable sense of his own worth and dignity with a peculiar dependence on the attitude of others to him. Even after "purification," Lear has no serenity or the sort of special wisdom that can attach to one who has been on a wheel of fire. This lack is evident when Lear is contrasted with Zossima or Oedipus of *Oedipus at Colonus*. Had Cordelia won the battle, one suspects that Lear would have been something of a trial and burden to her, as he sat with eyes glued to her every move. The "let's-away-to-prison" speech is rightly praised, but there was little future in it for Cordelia.

Humanities: Self-Containment of an Idea

Lear achieves greatness in this play not because suffering has transformed him into a Zossima; rather there is greatness in his suffering because it is a full though painful appreciation of the value of what he has lost.

Normally in tragedies there is a restoration of an ordered and moral world. In *King Lear* the "evil" elements are indeed purged, but the restoration is minimized. Indeed, the peculiar character of the tragedy is highlighted by an abortive ending. With the battle over, the sisters' deaths announced, and Gloucester's death reported, Albany treats these events much as the end of the action, giving judgment on them as if we were at the end of the play. Then Kent arrives and causes them to remember the "great thing of us forgot." Then comes the death of Cordelia. Thus, the restoration precedes that final tragic fact, so that attention focuses exclusively on it. And, as we have noted, the final comments are almost wholly on the ravages that all, especially Lear, have endured. His death is not at this point so much a consequence of the tragedy as a relief from it—as extreme a mode of catharsis as tragedy could discover, but one most proper to a tragedy of suffering.

EXTENSIONS OF THE IDEA

In our discussion of a scientific idea, we stressed the variations of development it lent itself to, whereas we have used the humanistic concept as an example of self-sufficiency within a single instance. The lines for development within the humanistic concept are similarly rich, but they are generated from quite different roots than those we saw in science. One method of development is rearranging elements. Thus, most tragedies have among their elements the moral character of the protagonist, the change he goes through, some sources of dehumanization or alienation, and his suffering. In *Lear* the suffering is made basic, and all the other elements are present as subordinate functions. But, clearly, other plays can make other elements basic. In *Oedipus,* for example, change is basic in the specific sense that the plot is so shaped that the total reversal of Oedipus' situation is made to hang on a single word and in that his situation is turned upside down in one instant—a reversal toward

121

which the prior action has led. The other elements remain but are subordinate; for example, suffering occurs after the reversal, rather than throughout the play. Or the focus of a play can be the nobility of the man who suffers and the extent to which the suffering is undeserved—in that case a martyr tragedy would result, as in *Beckett*. Or, if the process of dehumanization is basic, conceived in such extreme terms that it can be shown only as a disfiguration, then a tragedy of alienation results, as in Conrad's *Heart of Darkness*. In all these tragedies the four elements are present; but in each work one element is made the pivot around which the others turn.

This "fanning out" of the concept of tragedy is not like an alternative proof of the same theorem in science, but neither is it an indication that tragedy is loosely conceived. All four kinds of tragedy are included within the concept; they need to be added together, as it were (not merged, but entertained together). That each is itself true to the same root concept is shown by the presence in each one of the same four elements. Within this same frame, endless variations are possible. Thus, *The Sun Also Rises* centers from the beginning on Jake's suffering, making physical the impotence that was political in *King Lear*. Jake is no Lear, and therefore a different mode and structure of suffering are explored.

Such possibilities still do remain within a fairly restricted frame. The concept of tragedy is capable of still greater enlargements in its application to universal fields outside literature. The two most obviously universal fields are history and philosophy. H. J. Mueller interprets the course of history in the framework of tragedy in *Uses of the Past;* Unamuno reads the idea of tragedy into the nature of any action in the *Tragic Sense of Life*. Or, at the other extreme, Plato argues in the *Republic* that tragedy is false as a presentation of human nature.

However, we return from this fanning out of the concept back to the single case. This self-contained whole should not be reduced to the sort of unity provided by, for example, an opening in which an author says he will tell *a, b,* and *c.* When he has told of them, he has satisfied the measure he set up. But it is a measure mainly because he has decided to make it so; there need be no intrinsic unity in that *a-b-c* presentation. Rather author and audience agree to attend to this series. But the measure we have been examining in *Lear* is internal to the object presented. Because the beginning contains the seeds of its termination, the point-by-point reversal of the situation constitutes an autonomous whole.

History:
Reach of
an Idea

❧ 10 ❧

We have considered the autonomy of a scientific truth and a humanistic concept. To a limited extent we considered the connection of these ideas to their external context—how they were derived from experience and applied back to it. But our emphasis was on the internal structure of the ideas. Now, in order to focus on external connections, we turn to a third discipline, history, which by its nature makes that question central, since it is itself an inquiry into the way ideas arise from and interact with circumstances and situations.

We have chosen Herodotus' history as our example, not simply because he is likely to be widely known as a classic and the father of history, but also because he illustrates in an exemplary way the process by which ideas function in history as means of drawing out to the full the patterns that are in circumstances and situations. To help assure common understanding, most references will be to the first book (Clio), although other books will have to be referred to occasionally.

First we must guard against the easy temptation to impose our narrow historical criteria on him too quickly. Herodotus clearly believed in and shaped his history partly on the working of a divine nemesis. Although his historical subject required that he begin with

124

History: Reach of an Idea

Croesus, he went back to Gyges and traced the sequence of the whole dynasty, finding its downfall through Croesus to be a divine punishment for the transgression of Gyges. It is easy to say that this nemesis strand in Herodotus is not history but only a carry-over of religious or speculative thought into the infancy of history; this assumption is no doubt one of the reasons Hume said that "real history" did not begin until Thucydides.[1] Similarly, since Herodotus includes many an interesting story or custom which has little obvious or immediate relevance to the development of the main chain of events, we are tempted to dismiss them from the historical dimension and regard them as a poetic residue. Indeed, Herodotus' tendency to dwell on the heroism of actions or the importance of central figures can be seen as a vestige of the epic tradition. Finally, the work abounds with detailed descriptions of such places as Scythia and Egypt, giving the whole an encyclopedic air. Yet we must be wary of regarding these features as non-historical. No *a priori* edict outlaws them.

While we would have preferred to use here a simpler kind of work, to have done so could have operated against our purpose—namely, to see the working of ideas in or from the circumstantial context. It is the encyclopedic "irrelevancies" which make it evident that Herodotus gives a richer, and perhaps less sifted, account of the circumstantial context of the war than one usually finds in history, and as a result we have a better chance to see ideas or patterns emerge from them. Accordingly, we will suppose that Herodotus' conception of his work was that, *as* history (in Greek the word is the same—historia—that we translate today variously as "inquiry," "information," "record," "history"), it should contain such an open complex. This view is also justified by the epigraph, which reads: "These are the researches of Herodotus of Halicarnassus, which he publishes, in the hope of thereby preserving from decay the remembrance of what men have done, and of preventing the great and wonderful actions of the Greeks and the

[1] Quoted by J. Gavorse in his introduction to *Thucydides: The Peloponnesian War* (New York: Modern Library, 1934), p. xv.

Barbarians from losing their due meed of glory; and withal to put on record what were their grounds of feud."[2]

The subjects he names are stated broadly enough to cover all the "irrelevancies," both in scope (the doings of men) and quality (glory); yet all are grouped as the researches (*historia*). Further, he suggests that all are tied to the quarrel in the opening sentence of the history as well: "According to the Persians best informed in history, the Phoenicians began the quarrel" (I, 1). We will argue the relations of these subjects later, only wishing now to establish a presumption of a concept of history in which the most diverse doings of men have to be noted as part of the circumstantial and moral environment of a single war.

This presumption is suggested by additional self-conscious remarks by Herodotus. On the one hand, he speaks as if the subject is narrow: he is "compelled" by the "course of my history" to take up a given subject next (I, 37), and on the other hand he remarks, before noting a strange fact about the mules in Elis, "additions being what my work always from the very first affected" (IV, 213). Similarly, he can be historical in the narrow sense of presifting stories (for example, the accounts of Cyrus' rise) and presenting only the one he thinks true (I, 38), while in other cases he presents various versions and says: "For myself, my duty is to report all that is said; but I am not obliged to believe it all alike—a remark which may be understood to apply to my whole History" (VII, 403). The last remark presumably applies to cases about which Herodotus feels that the truth is not clear.

The presumption then is that the quarrel is the center and that a full historical view must see it as emergent from the complex of situations, peoples, wonders, and stories that form its circumstantial context. Let us note now how Herodotus builds this view. As he moves from country to country, he purports to offer a description of each. But instead of looking for the political, cultural, and military factors as such, in the systematic way Thucydides would, he looks simply for what is notable, wonderful, or strange. Further,

[2] *The History of Herodotus,* G. Rawlinson, trans. (New York: Tudor Press, 1928), Book I, p. 1.

the norm against which the notable is selected is not a sociological average as much as the Greek customs and methods. Thus, he spends little time on the Lydians, because they "have very nearly the same customs as the Greeks" (I, 37). To make these judgments he does not have to have a sharply articulated structure of what is "Greek" to use as a yardstick. Rather, he must himself be so Greek that anything significantly different among the Barbarians strikes him sharply. Thus, he begins with the idea of difference as an intellectual germ—a way of discovering what the difference really is. Had he approached the countries with antecedent knowledge about political or social structures, he might well have missed the features that carry the key or *gestalt* of the people. Indeed, the more structured the idea of "Greek" initially, the more likely that an alien framework of contrast would be imposed on the Barbarians.

In applying this heuristic principle of difference, Herodotus' method is generally a liberal search for patterns—liberal in the sense that he does not test to see whether a preconceived pattern is present, but rather to see whether the facts selected out by the principle of difference cause one to emerge. It is this use of the criterion of patterning that is important. Take the first case: The Lydians (Croesus) lie between the Greeks and Persians, and this bare geographical fact reflects and partly causes the pattern of their relations. The Lydians have a middle-man status. Thus, the Lydians are the first Asiatics to commit aggressions against the Greeks, but when the Persians attack the Lydians, the latter seek to ally themselves with Greeks and even consult the Greek oracles. Similarly, the Lydian customs are nearly like the Greek customs on the one hand, but on the other, the chief wonder Herodotus notes is the enormous size of the tomb of Alyattes, the father of Croesus. The reader is struck by this Barbarian-like glorification of the single leader, since by this time we have heard Solon deprecate the *hubris* of Croesus (anticipating that of the Barbarian autocrat generally). Finally, this recurrent pattern of the Lydians' intermediate status between Greek and Barbarian is embodied (almost too perfectly) in the relationships of Solon, Croesus, and Cyrus. Solon's view is set against Croesus' view when Solon makes his fictitious visit to Croesus. Then

127

when Croesus is defeated, he becomes convinced that Solon was right. He becomes the adviser to Cyrus and proceeds thereafter to give him Solonic advice. In brief—Solon:Croesus::Croesus: Cyrus. The Lydian is the perfect mean. This intermediate pattern emerges wherever one touches the Lydian portion of the history— in military and diplomatic relations, religious bases, ideology, custom, and geographic relations. (With the fall of the Lydians, the variability in the situation disappears, since the dropping out of this middle causes the extremes to meet.)

Thus, from the inductive use of the principle of difference, a specific pattern emerges, itself containing germs for further development, as in the idea of autocracy suggested by Croesus' initial situation. This suggestion is what Herodotus follows up next. Leaving Lydia, he turns to the precursors of Cyrus for background. This begins when the Medes, after having enjoyed "the blessings of self-government," fell again "under the sway of kings in a manner which I will now relate" (I, 38). Herodotus proceeds to tell how Deioces conceived and carried out his design to obtain the sovereign power. The method is again to begin with an open heuristic idea and build a pattern. It is almost as if Deioces is himself a historian/agent. He has a basic belief "that justice and injustice are engaged in a perpetual conflict" (I, 38). Herodotus cannot detail this idea for us but rather shows how Deioces uses it to uncover and exploit situations. As judge, he so arranges matters that, while injustice occurs spontaneously, the administration of justice is outside the scope of private individuals or of groups as such and so depends on him as someone above or distant from the swirl of private conflicts. Once he is made king, this elevation of himself outside normal processes is given symbolic form (no subjects can have direct access to or even view him). What has emerged is a definite pattern of events and relations constitutive of an autocracy, as a result of the way a man uses the idea of the justice/injustice opposition to distance himself from all others. The pattern is developed further in the history as new rulers up to Xerxes enter. And the Greek political nature is suggested by use of the principle of difference: Book I's view of Athens, for example, highlights the ineffective and hectic swirl of

128

events that attend the vain efforts of the Pisistratus family to con-
solidate autocratic control.

We have come far enough to see that ideas are being used
not as imposable patterns but as plastic possibilities that bend to
the circumstances in which they are actualized. The autonomy of
the inquiry consists in its having within itself the constituents needed
for this process. The idea of *justice* as used here is not autonomous,
but the process by which it is shaped to the structure of a benevolent
and incipiently Xerxes-like tyranny is.

It remains now to note some of the broader patterns in which
the encyclopedic strands noted earlier are involved. Let us consider
"the quarrel." Herodotus says in the epigraph, it will be recalled,
that he will put its grounds on record. We believe it would be a
serious error, one that goes against the patterning method of the
work, to believe that this statement refers to the casual antecedents
of the war. When Thucydides speaks of the causes of a war, he
refers to what led up to it, but Herodotus' focus is on the broader-
gauged fact that when the war between the Greeks and Persians
is *finished,* then, as in any feud, the causes of feud are greater than
they were before. And when the opposition of philosophic perspectives as well as customs is added to the wars that fuel the feud, then
the entire history is an account of the grounds that *now* make the
Greeks and Barbarians enemies.

In this light, the movement of the history is in accord with
the growth of the difference between Greek and Barbarian from a
miniscule incident in history into the dominant fact of the times.
The work begins with a reported account of the quarrel, over a
woman, of a few Greeks and Phoenicians at the boundary between
the two worlds. Embedded in this minor altercation we already have
the principle of difference operating. It seems absurd to the Barbarians that the Greeks would go to war over a woman. And soon the
last of the Heraclids, Candaules, king of Lydia, is suffering the consequences of treating his wife as desirable property rather than as a
person. This germ in an ethical issue develops into the war between
Croesus and the Asiatic Greeks and then enlarges into the philosophic difference between Croesus and Solon; but in the total sweep

of events this altercation still seems a small matter. Cyrus does not
regard the Asiatic Greeks as worth his attention. He sends deputies
to wage war on them while he himself proceeds to larger ends. The
encounters of the Persians with the Massagetae, Egypt, and so on,
then develop. But as Persia swells, so also do her collisions and
threats of collision with the Greeks grow. The opposition widens
and deepens until it becomes the consuming passion of the Persian
leaders and the overriding concern of the Greeks. Finally, it over-
arches the whole ancient world.

The ending of the work marks the stabilization of the feud,
not its end, since events, social structure, and philosophic perspectives alike show why neither party can overcome the other. The
Greek counterattack dissipates from the lack of cohesion and drive
that a single command might have provided, while conversely,
Xerxes cannot mount another effective invasion because of the
corruptions that attend the exercise of an unquestioned single command. But it is now more clear, and more historically warranted,
that the feud is total.

Without the broader circumstantial context of "what men
have done" and of the various countries with which Persia became
involved, the significance of the Greek-Persian opposition would
be lost. Any of the other quarrels were candidates for becoming the
dominant fact of history. But the principle of difference—operative
in the manner of "wonderful" actions or in whatever men do (Cyrus
took the fact that the Greeks gathered together to trade and cheat in
the marketplace as the significant clue to the kind of war they would
wage)—and the principle of patterning enabled Herodotus to see,
and history to become, an opposition of Greek and Barbarian.

The assumptions operative in so complex a work are too
numerous to cover here. But we have sought to show that initial
assumptions about such objects as justice, the Greek way, freedom,
tyranny, and so on, function as heuristic devices that get their meaning from their workings in the historical context. Space and time
become important considerations in such a context. Time is not
understood as a sequence of literally equal intervals, but as cumulative; the situation at the beginning of the work is relatively open; at

130

the end it is heavy with the remembrance of what men have done and the shape their deeds give the present. Similarly, space is not a grid of equal segments, but is more like an originally undifferentiated surface on which people and events rise up as centers or pivots.

As complete as it is for its own purpose, Herodotus' history gives us only one variant of the process we are seeking here to illustrate. Our concern in this chapter, it will be remembered, is with the way ideas interact with circumstantial contexts to create an autonomous structure. There are two directions in which this interaction can occur: first is Herodotus' paradigm of the use of principles to cause ideas or patterns to emerge from the context. The second direction is toward applying—"imposing"—ideas on phenomena.

While Herodotus follows the first direction, Edward Gibbon follows the second, developing his history as an application of scientific ideas and categories to circumstances. This method resembles the kind of applications of scientific ideas already discussed in an earlier section; but we need to note certain special features that enter when the application is historical. Gibbon says his design is "to deduce the most important circumstances" of the decline and fall of the Roman Empire.[3] Our task is to make clear what this sort of deduction is.

At the beginning of his discussion of the Roman constitution, Gibbon typically introduces the nonhistorical theory that is to serve as his frame for analysis: "A martial nobility and stubborn commons, possessed of arms, tenacious of property, and collected into constitutional assemblies, form the only balance capable of preserving a free constitution against enterprises of an aspiring prince" (p. 53). The contrast with Herodotus is of course sharp. Gibbon's frame of reference is a literal law, applicable to any people, and based on a conception of the universal categories of a stable polity.

The application of the law to history, however, does not

[3] Edward Gibbon, *The Decline and Fall of the Roman Empire* (New York: Modern Library), p. 1.

consist in noting the law's instantiation or embodiment. On the contrary, where such a balanced constitution, as described in the law existed, there would in a sense be no constitutional history; for the basic tendency of the operation of the law is to maintain stability by equilibrium and balance of power. But history is change rather than repeated regularities. It is also change for Herodotus, but for him the change marks the coming to fruition of seeds of unity; for Gibbon, the changes making up history mark the violations of the laws of politicosocial regularities. Thus, while he employs scientific theory as his frame of analysis, the result is to show that history "is, indeed, little more than the register of the crimes, follies, and misfortunes of mankind" (p. 69). Let us see how this operates in the case of the imperial constitution. Augustus established what was in fact "an absolute monarchy disguised by the forms of a commonwealth" (p. 61). That his governance has this form follows from the law in that Augustus carefully preserved the senate and even tolerated the assembly. But the system was only a form because the essential attribute of the nobility and commons named in the law (they are martial and possessed of arms) was separated off; the constitution is now composed of four elements—prince, senate, people, and the army—instead of the three named in the law; this separation of the military marked the end of Roman liberty. We have been formalistic in describing Gibbon's analysis in order to accentuate the way the law both governs the analysis (since it names all the relevant factors and their stable mode of combination) and at the same time gives way to the facts (that is, the different ways the factors were, in fact, associated).

This redistribution of factors sets up the probability of decline, since the system is now destabilized, and provides the basis for "deducing" the circumstances of that decline. As Gibbon proceeds to recount the reigns of successive emperors, he seeks out any changes in the relative status of army, senate, and people. He knows in advance that when even the appearance of senatorial authority is erased, he can deduce the next major step in the decline.

Of course, there are many variant ways by which historians discover sequences in circumstances. For example, Trotsky, in *The*

Russian Revolution, finds the critical events to be those that match politicocultural forms to new "objective" conditions. This approach differs from Herodotus' organization of the conditions into patterns, as well as Gibbon's measure of conditions by antecedent theory. Herodotus and Gibbon represent extremes in the adjustment of ideas of history to circumstances and are therefore singled out here.

In the preceding chapters on scientific and humanistic ideas, we argued that their truth or adequacy is not to be conveyed by authority or preferential opinion. In the way we set up this explanation in the preceding chapters, it probably would not be disputed, since it focuses on the internal structure and development of ideas. The dispute would tend to arise at the points where the claim is made that an idea varies according to circumstances or gets its meaning from its applicability to life. This argument is sometimes considered hostile to the autonomy of ideas, for it immerses them realistically in the flux of life. This immersion gives them a certain variability and relativity. Every idea of course has a relativistic dimension, but this final section demonstrates that this relativistic dimension also can be made the subject of inquiry and communication; its claim to validity rests on the autonomy achievable in the inquiry. This dimension is an appropriate one to close on here, for it may be useful in the student's use of the fruits of university study as he encounters problems and circumstances in his life beyond the university.

Extended Issues

❦ FOUR ❦

Part Four is an exploration of various extended issues that are not caused so much by pressures for immediate particular change (as in Part Two) but are issues of more scope, requiring longer-range conceptions and plans.

A development of these extended issues provides additional occasions for using the principles stated in Part One to analyze diverse aspects of university activity. The first issue is how to construct a flexible but comprehensive program of courses in one of the broad curriculum areas. We suggest such a program for the humanities (Chapter Eleven), although we make no claim that this program is the only one that can achieve this objective. Second (Chapter Twelve), we explore the notion of teaching methods to show the intimate relation of effective method with the development of subject matter in the classroom. And finally (Chapter Thirteen), we consider the limits inherent in classroom activity. The argument of the book is thus brought from general principles to an indication of the flexibility of programs consonant with them and of the ultimate limits of classroom instruction.

Structuring

a

Curriculum

ᘏᗢᘏ 11 ᘏᗢᘏ

In the preceding chapters we have illustrated the autonomy of ideas with deliberately restricted examples—adequate simply to show that the development of an idea is rooted in a rigorously logical internal power as well as in the imagination or manipulation of those who inquire into it and use it. On this base we wish now to suggest the way in which such criteria of disciplinary autonomy can be expanded to much broader problems of curriculum and indeed recast in interdisciplinary terms.

We do not claim that an interdisciplinary approach is more appropriate than a disciplinary one, just as in the preceding examples we did not claim the converse. The key is in the integrity and perspicuity of subject matter. Often the distinction between what belongs to a discipline and what is shared by two is either a historical accident, awaiting the development of a new discipline, or only an apparent sharing, since each may make an integral whole out of the aspect of the problem with which it is concerned. A field of study has defensible scope if it deals with an isolated problem.

But a concern for nuclear subjects should not be rigidified into the view that education consists of a collection of atomlike, separable units. Independent inquiries must themselves be linked up in larger coherent chains. Earlier examples illustrated that an inquiry is fenced off for stated purposes in a stated context, and in earlier arguments we noted how a given restricted subject matter opens up lines of inquiry beyond its immediate scope. But merely to assert the need for interrelations is excessively abstract and platitudinous. This need can be given content by devising a model curricular plan which, in fact, links separable disciplines and subjects without blurring the differences among them.

There have been many curricula of wider scope than the ones presented here. For example, the liberal arts of the medieval curriculum—the trivium of grammar, rhetoric, and logic, and the quadrivium of arithmetic, geometry, music, and astronomy—formed a secular unity compatible with philosophic and religious studies. The undergraduate program of the College of University of Chicago in the years following World War II was made up of an organized structure of courses, roughly the same for all students, which was in itself a total bachelor's degree program divided (and united) by a systematic view of the major fields of knowledge. Harvard in the postwar years moved in the same direction—that is, providing a unity of liberal arts distinguished by their subject matters (rather than by methods, as in the medieval trivium)—but restricted this structure to a common core on the basis of which students moved off into specialized areas. The program we present is more limited, in that it is restricted to the humanities, but nevertheless it seeks functional cross-links within the context of its limited purpose.[1]

The particular purpose of the program is to provide a humanistic base for students specializing in one field of the humanities, so that they can become aware of the versatility and depth of their specialized work and recognize the potential reach of any one field. Kinds of rigor vary deliberately within the program, for even methods of reasoning must be adapted to subject and purpose. Indeed, as the original plan for this program has operated in practice, the tendency has been to emphasize the differences of method: that is, to focus successively on the *rhetorical* questions of innovating

[1] This scheme is one of several developed by various liberal arts institutions for their Humanities program.

or stabilizing ideas and practices (in the first course); on the *analytic* questions of part and whole in the second; on the *logical* questions raised by chains of thought (feeling) in the third; and, finally, on the *dialectical* questions of relating thought to action, in the fourth. (The nature and differences of these methods will become clearer below.)

CORE PROGRAM IN THE HUMANITIES

Study of one special field such as philosophy or English literature requires corollary study in the general area of the humanities to provide a context that enlarges perception and makes possible more responsible choices and judgments.

To introduce the program we consider first the general concept of the humanities and the problems associated with it. The humanities share a concern with what is specifically human. But they do not depend on a fixed definition of human nature. Their interest is in its manifestation in works of philosophy, literature, rhetoric, and art, and also in works which defy these categories, all conceived and explored as intellectual and imaginative constructs. Together they constitute the common subject matter of the humanities, common in that they are diverse manifestations of the same creative source.

The recognition of this identity has led in the past to Great Books courses and other similar general humanities courses ordered chronologically. At times, they have been so unstructured, however, as to become a series of impressionistic responses or a vehicle for some historical thesis about past cultures. A suitable program for our ends, while based on the same material, has to be more structured. Since full coverage is impossible, the organizational focus is, rather, on autonomous ideas as they are developed in the context of three primary problems in a humanistic education.

The first problem arises from the richness of the works that make up the subject matter of the humanities. For example, no single perspective is adequate to *War and Peace,* neither the conventional specialized literary scholarship, nor embracing ideological criticism. Each perspective can be adequate to its sphere of interest but not to the work itself. In order to do justice to the work it is necessary to confront the student with the full range of relevant disciplines, yet to do so in such a way as to separate and juxtapose them sharply so that the peculiar illuminating powers of each perspective can emerge. Thus, although the range is interdisciplinary, the treatment of each aspect is strictly in accord with the relevant specialized field.

There are evident values in cutting across disciplines. Key ideas such as freedom receive profound treatment in works of history, literature, philosophy, and related disciplines; and significant variables in the problem can be overlooked without some attention to the way these treatments supplement or otherwise relate to each other.

The second problem concerns method of thought. There is a danger of oversimplifying the methods of the humanities. Thus, C. P. Snow groups humanistic discipline such as philosophy, literature, and art together as constituting the "literary culture," which is thought to have a single nonrigorous method—that is, the men of the literary culture proceed intuitively, subjectively, imaginatively. This unsystematic method is contrasted with the methods of fact-finding and objective proof employed by the scientist. Too often this view is so interpreted that it sets up one model of rigor, assuming that imaginative thought is inherently sloppy even if sometimes rewarding. A second flaw is the merging of methods of the different humanistic disciplines—assuming, for example, that because speculative philosophy does not depend on empirical experiments it is but another form of poetry. In the proposed program the distinctive kinds of argument and insight relevant to the different disciplines, and the different bases of autonomy that each claims, are explored. As a result we develop a conception of diverse kinds of rigor, each to be judged by its adequacy to the problem being treated.

The third problem concerns the student. His judgments and choices, especially in the humanities, depend in good measure on the diverse kinds of analysis or response that he has at his command.

It is therefore essential not only that he have studied this or that list of objective works, but also that he have developed certain analytic and intuitive powers.

FORMAL RELATIONS OF COURSES

The courses making up the program are: I. Interdisciplinary concepts; II. Disciplines: art; III. Disciplines: philosophy; IV. Values: historical and intellectual. These four units provide a full scheme of relations among the fields. Unit I, in dealing with topics common to all the humanities, explores the unity of the area. Units II and III deal with separate disciplines and so seek to isolate excellences peculiar to each. Unit IV deals with values, sometimes common to several disciplines, sometimes elevated in one, and thus advances to the point where the organization of the area as an intelligible structure can be considered.

The treatment of the four units forms a comparable scheme. Unit I focuses on topics that have had momentous import for man (for example, commitment and loyalty), recurring not only from epoch to epoch but in field after field. The method of examining these topics is *rhetorical*—that is, the works are often treated less in their own terms than as instruments for generating thought. The disciplinary method used in Units II and III treats the demands made by the nature of the work itself and the demands that the work itself seeks to make on its studies. Thus, Unit II looks at art in terms of how it is derived from experience and how it forms an esthetic object analyzable in a whole-part relationship. Unit III looks at works of philosophy and other discursive disciplines for the patterns and principles they exhibit in shaping the problems of man. Unit IV, finally, moves to the broader organizations of knowledge and art, and thus treats disciplines *dialectically*—that is, each work is judged by its role in a larger intellectual or historical context.

SPECIFIC CONTENT

Interdisciplinary concepts. The first course in the program assumes a standard level of taste in its students and some background in humanistic works. The goal of the first unit is to extend the range of this commonality and give it some initial order so that a sense of the autonomous potentialities of the humanistic disciplines begins to open up for the student.

The various perspectives from which works in different disciplines can be seen as a unity provide the topics of the course. Works of literature, philosophy, and visual art are employed to develop a theme—for instance, the theme of commitment or piety: Antigone, Socrates, Job, Christ, Camus' *The Stranger* and others.

Questions of form will also be relevant. For example, in the consideration of Antigone's and Socrates' giving up their lives out of commitment to a transpolitical principle, it becomes evident that Antigone's action is *tragic* and that she so responds to it, while Socrates' is not and he does not so respond. The works show that the concept of piety developed in *Antigone* is itself appropriate to an imaginative work, while Socrates' response is related to the philosophic character of the *Apology*.

Subsequent topics shift from works considered as thematic to works considered as merging in a common effort to break through custom (theater of the absurd, existentialist philosophy), or conversely, as unified by the effort to achieve stability in tradition (for example, the Hippolytus story from Euripides to O'Neill), or finally, as organized by the effort to move a community to action (*A Modest Proposal, The Communist Manifesto*). These topics are meant to be illustrative primarily. Other possibilities might be the idea of "God," or "tragedy" seen as an idea that orders literary, artistic, and philosophic perceptions. The topics have an intelligible sequence: the first is ideological; the second and third are historical; the fourth, rhetorical.

The work of art. The chief arts tend to be differentiated by their materials—music by sounds, visual art by sights, and so on. Direct confrontation of such materials and study of theories can open up problems and controversy, however. Is optical color the same as aesthetic color? Are sounds colorful, and do colors sound? Does the stone of sculptures of persons "represent" flesh? Thus, the first section of the course explores the aesthetics of materials in direct experience, the exploration being stimulated by arguments of men

141

such as Plato, Lessing, Croce, Sartre, and Moore. However, direct experience of art, as well as theory, soon develops problems in the enjoyment of pure form. If too pure, form seems to pall; tension and variety are sought as well as symmetry and balance. In the second section of the course, this question of beauty as imperfect form can be given its complexity in a range of materials from sonnets and simple abstract painting to Homer and Michelangelo.

Finally, in our experience of art we often do not abstract the matter and the form. It is the union of the two that causes our response. The union is more than a simple sum of the two; even a chemical compound has properties not in the elements.

In art, however, the synthesis goes further. It reacts upon and affects the elements. For example, the language of *Oedipus Rex* in itself carries a pure sensuous delight, but the language is also noble and terrifying in order to mirror the man who utters it. The shape of the plot, as formal design, has a pleasing symmetry accompanied by the titillations of ironic twists and turns; but as the soul of the drama, the shape of the plot is terrifying for it creates the total and sudden turning upside down of a man's world.

The nature of the work, as a work of art, rests in the special power it has as a synthesis of all its elements, a power pervading and affecting those elements, often to the point of generating a new set of "parts," such as spectacle, discovery, and poetic vision. The third section analyzes the way elements converge to create this power in works such as *Paradise Lost, Guernica,* Joyce's *Ulysses,* and *Threepenny Opera.*

Philosophy (argument). Argument is treated as the process of drawing out the results of principles; its prime exemplars are found in philosophic classics such as Plato's *Republic,* Aristotle's *Ethics,* Lucretius' *On the Nature of Things,* and St. Augustine's *Confessions.* These works differ in literary form, and nothing could more dramatically illustrate the power of a principle than the relation between the philosophic bases of these works and their form; for example, the theory of knowledge in the *Republic* requires dialogue; Aristotle's assumption of discrete subject matters justifies his didactic lecture form; and knowledge emerges for St. Augustine in autobiography—specifically, confession. Thus, consideration of literary form generates questions of method: from dialogue to dialectic; from lecture to analysis; from confession before God to a spiritual rhetoric.

The classics of philosophy selected for the first section of Unit III need not—in fact, should not—have the same subject matters; for in the realm of reason the subject matter chosen for major treatment should not merely be a subject one happens to find interesting, but rather the subject made fundamental by one's approach or method. That Plato talks of politics while Lucretius centers on physics is a function of their metaphysics.

In this exploration of the power of reason, the range of possible topics is so great that a focusing device is required, if only for practical reasons. The safest source of control is in adhering to the evolution of the argument in each case and seeking the necessities of its movement from link to link. This focus on the *movement* of argument is an effort to reconstruct the inquiry.

In the second section of this unit, the role of reason is examined in less abstract occurrences—that is, in the polemics of politics, in poetic theory, in history. The problem here is in part to disentangle the bases of argument from other considerations; therefore, the mode of inquiry must accordingly shift from simply following an argument to pinpointing differences of position and probing the nature of the opposition. Through such inquiry, what appears to be an opposition of fact, or interest, turns out to be also, or perhaps instead, a compatible difference in the autonomous bases of the key ideas.

The debates between Lincoln and Douglas may be reduced by historians to group interests, but the speeches themselves rest on differences in the conception of human nature and of the relation of theory and practice. Wordsworth and Coleridge in their discussion of poetry do not simply have opposed reactions to the language of rustics; their opposed conceptions of philosophy itself give different meaning to the conception of language, poetry, and rustic life. The histories of Herodotus and Thucydides cross paths in the pre-Persian history of Athens and Sparta; their radically different versions of the "same" material carries back to differences in the nature and causes of power and national growth, not to a simple difference between objective and mythical history. Darwin's theory of pangenesis and Weismann's germ-plasm theory show how, when scientists are projecting areas for fruitful research in relatively unknown realms, their principles—not just their hunches—help light the way.

The third section concentrates on a contemporary problem bypassed by the preceding sections. Whereas the first section followed the way in which a principle establishes itself, and the second examined uses of such principles in special fields, the third moves to language as the locus or source from which principles are drawn in contemporary thought. For example, some scholars, like Cassirer and Heidegger, make names and naming basic; others, like Wittgenstein and Carnap, center on propositions. Within each pair, other diversities develop. Thus, Cassirer finds in original names the undifferentiated primitive precursors of more substantial and more focused insights and achievements, while Heidegger finds in original naming the key philosophic insights which can be lost by efforts at decisive systemization. Similarly, Wittgenstein finds basic the propositions of ordinary language, while Carnap seeks to go beyond its obscurities by constructing a logical syntax. The general point made throughout this section, however, is the availability of language today for supplying new principles to be established and applied.

Values and judgments. This course turns to the nature and diversity of values. The prior curriculum, taken as embodied humanistic values, provides the background of data on which this course reflects. The subject of value needs to be keyed to the specific problem of a general humanities curriculum, the problem of judgment of the works and arts of man. In the natural sciences one does not judge the worth of the speed of light, and there is minimal concern for each case as an entity. But no contact with a work of man is adequate without a judgment of its worth as an individual instance of human expression. And the ultimate source of this judgment lies not only in the work being judged but also in the values of the judge himself.

Structuring a Curriculum

Accordingly, the course should be organized in sections, with each section exploring a given value term (such as tragedy) and its changes in meaning and scope as the valuer or judge shifts point of view. As an example of one complete section let us take the case given—tragedy. Aristotle's *Poetics* treats it as a purely aesthetic concept that provides a basis for making a play; Nietzsche's *Birth of Tragedy* retains the aesthetic cast but makes tragedy the fundamental power of man, suggesting that all values lie in art. Unamuno's *Tragic Sense of Life* shares Nietzsche's sense of the scope and power of tragedy but frees it from its aesthetic orientation; for him, the birth of tragedy would occur, not when the dramatists developed it, but the first time a man dreaded death. Finally, Croce, in his *Aesthetic,* provides the student with an entirely new perspective on tragedy. By treating tragedy as essentially indistinguishable from comedy, Croce challenges assumptions underlying all of the preceding arguments.

Similarly, other sections would show such shifts in the widening and narrowing of value terms in other disciplines: the question of freedom in history (for example, Hegel's *Reason and History* or McKeon's *Freedom and History*); and of knowledge in philosophy (for example, Plato's *Phaedo* and Russell's "A Free Man's Worship").

What are the effects hoped for from such a program? It is not intended that the student develop some overarching cultural synthesis. The primary emphasis is on his discovery of diverse values as well as diverse capacities in himself to be actively engaged with those values. The richness of the experience and of the results depends on the diversity of the autonomous activities involved. Nonetheless as we have seen, the program is not made up of a random succession of courses. Integration is aimed for, but in limited ways. The activities are set in a scheme which makes the transition from one to another understandable, which opens up lines of connection that can themselves become the focus of new inquiries, and which finally is itself made the object of an independent inquiry.

Teaching
Methods

⋘ 12 ⋙

The distinction of subject matter (as something external) from methods of teaching and learning (as psychological processes) is generally out of favor today. But too often the result is that the students' supposed psychological needs are given overbalanced priority—as when programmers indiscriminately atomize knowledge into memorizable chunks or when formal restraints or rules are thrown off to accommodate the mind's need to be free. Since we have been concerned with showing the priority and nature of the autonomous ideas on which university activity should turn, it may appear that we have given overbalanced attention to subject matter. However, the appearance is misleading, for the concept of autonomous ideas itself cuts across the distinction of content and psychological process. An idea is *ipso facto* a psychological entity; an autonomous idea has an intrinsic content to unfold. Accordingly, in a sense we have been concerned with method throughout as involved in the "push" of ideas. But our chief focus has been on what emerges from the push rather than on the senses in which it is "method."

In this chapter we look directly at questions of method, specifically at those which have been highlighted in the current ferment and psychological research. Although our discussion ranges from a concern with internalized learning to the downgrading of grades, we do not attempt to cover all problems, and we are pleased that much of practical value is being provided by some of the

146

studies done from a psychosocial point of view. But that perspective suffers from lack of contact with the structure of ideas involved. Our intention is to show some of the effects of this bias, and our main intention in the chapter, accordingly, is to indicate how the ideational point of view provides useful guides to classroom method. We do not deny that the student ferment has been catalyzed—and has been given greater plausibility—by weaknesses in the methods employed in many university classrooms today. In what follows, we take issue with the classroom's critics, not in order to claim that all is well, but rather to clear the way for a more specific and useful identification of methodological difficulties than is currently provided.

SELF-DIRECTED LEARNING

Michael Rossman has given broad social significance to current dissatisfaction with the method of the classroom: it follows an "American style"—the "authority complex"—that "permeates our culture." Authority is typically exercised in America as a function of fixed roles in a hierarchical system; and the university classroom is a model of this process because it is "authority-centered."[1] The new education would develop the student's capacity for self-direction. In the simplest forms of antiauthoritarianism, this new goal results in the call for unregulated independent projects or free-form group interactions. We will deal with such university-level variants of Summerhill subsequently. First, we wish to consider the more limited and more sophisticated variants of the new education made from the behavioral point of view. The behavioristic views rest on one overarching premise—namely, that the knowledge or understanding that is most effectively one's own is that which is generated from within oneself; knowledge that is externally introduced tends to be alien or only mechanically known. As a result, internalized learning develops innovative individuals who can think for themselves. Students without such experience in learning "are so used to having the professor tell them what to do that, if you

[1] Michael Rossman, "Learning and Social Change: The Problem of Authority," in P. Runkel, R. Harrison, and M. Runkel (Eds.), *The Changing College Classroom* (San Francisco: Jossey-Bass, 1969), pp. 25, 27.

give them a project, they wait around for someone to tell them how to do it. . . ."[2]

According to the new approach, the alternative to this approach to learning is to "expose the learner to a variety of experiences, events, facts, and phenomena, expecting that he will find the relationships, categories, and concepts that order and explain his experience."[3] This method can also be applied to the development of deductive processes; the student is left on his own to apply theories. The new approach is in rapport with our own, for in seeing how a concept explains relations, a student can also grasp an aspect of its autonomy. We question, however, the internalist principle that an answer or truth effectively becomes a student's own only when he finds it within. In our view it is his own if he can take intellectual responsibility for it—that is, if he regards it as a truthful solution to a problem and can go on to defend and use it. Asked whether it is true or valuable, he need not cite his professor or retreat to "it's my opinion," but he is capable of offering argument. And if objections arise, from within himself or without, he does not depend on repetition of the given proof but goes beyond it to cope with the objections on their own terms, showing a command of the idea underyling the proof. Finally (and ideally), he can use the idea to open up new lines of inquiry.

By defining the test of "having" an idea as intellectual responsibility, we can see that the classroom must do more than simply turn the student to his own resources. At many points the authority and his expertise are needed to make a difficulty come alive as an intelligible difficulty. Sometimes the source of the answer is of little importance, provided one is ready for it. There are times when a much-sought answer just pops into one's head, but if an expert had instead uttered it at just this crucial moment, one could vouch for it nonetheless. Thus we see the art of teaching not as the art of telling or withholding a solution, but as the art of generating readiness.

[2] Roger Harrison, "Classroom Innovation: A Design Primer," *loc. cit.*, quoting an American on European-trained chemists, p. 310.
[3] *Ibid.*, p. 308.

Teaching Methods

Once the importance of readiness and responsibility is recognized, one can take a flexible view of what discovery and invention are. In team thinking, when the group has developed a common sense of a difficulty, and one man then breaks through it by excitedly offering a solution, the other members of the group are discovering too (from the standpoint of education, not of giving credit). The process of discovery in this sense could go on as well in productive listening or reading. Henri Poincaré calls this experience an illusion but nonetheless sees it as valid: "It seems to me . . . in repeating a reasoning learned, that I could have invented it. This is often only an illusion; but even then, even if I am not so gifted as to create it by myself, I myself re-invent it in so far as I repeat it."[4]

SOCIAL STRUCTURE OF THE CLASSROOM

Another major objection to the authoritarian style of teaching is that it inhibits free and honest communication. The anti-authoritarian view sees the classroom as set up to nourish the professor's ego and preserve his power, so remedies are often sought in restyling designed to reduce status barriers. It is said, for example, that all persons should be on a first-name basis; that there should be circular or other seating arrangements so that no one is at the head of the class; that the group meet in a lounge or on a hillside; and so on. State University of New York had a statewide conference on the teacher-learner relationship in 1969 that devoted much thought to such efforts to set up barrier-free communication. And recently at Stony Brook a complex survey has been initiated on the first-name question alone as a possible way of improving student-faculty relations; the survey explores the correlation between one's political views and one's form of address.

Power status too is considered relevant to classroom style. The student's equality in university governance and in hiring/firing influence is thought to give him the "clout" that will cause his opinions to be listened to with respect.

[4] Henri Poincaré, "Mathematical Creation," in B. Ghiselin (Ed.), *The Creative Process* (New York: New American Library, 1952), p. 35.

149

The Voiceless University

This egalitarian approach to classroom method seems to be but a special application of the general approach recommended by the American Council on Education's Special Committee on Campus Tension.[5] This blue-ribbon committee said that the prime need was to set up better lines of communication among the various "constituencies," since so much of the difficulty lay in the "behavior and attitudes" of one constituency as perceived by another. Thus, the committee also saw political relations and social manners as the locus of the problem.

These matters obviously are peripheral. The antiauthoritarian view is many cuts above Menenius' judgment that the best time to talk with Coriolanus was after Coriolanus had had a good breakfast, but they nonetheless are similar in approach. At best, they provide the external conditions for that internal development of ideas with which the classroom is concerned. This internal need primarily governs the question of the desirability and even definition of authority. We see the professor as an expert who retains the credibility of his credentials only by the communicable force of his ideas. He is someone under whose guidance the subject—or even his point of view on it—comes to speak for itself. Consequently, as we argued in Chapter Two, he is dependent on interaction with the minds of others. Friendly relations among persons may smooth the way for this process, but the authority of cogent argument generates it, and critical learners sustain it.

More directly pertinent than personal and political relations is the general preference today for small discussion groups over the lecture method. But there are difficulties here: the terms under discussion tend to take their meaning from the same external considerations we have noted—that is, the criterion that everyone get a hearing. This approach may be practical in the conduct of public affairs, but classroom communication obviously cannot be conducted on this model in a university. And even when "dialogue" is set up as the model, the purpose usually is to enable each "constituency" or individual to get to understand the point of view and interests of the other better.

[5] Reported in the *New York Times,* April 26, 1970.

150

Teaching Methods

We have doubts about how useful it is to compare the merits of "lecture," "dialogue," and so on simply as formal arrangements. Their value is relative to too many variables in purposes or in the character of the ideas being developed. Socrates is often thought of as the exemplar of the dialogue method of teaching and so he was, in principle. But, in fact, the actual practice involved his use of disparate methods. In the *Symposium,* he is one of a series of speechmakers, each giving his point of view in turn. In most of the *Republic* he proceeds by question and answer, but for the most part the answer he wants and gets is a simple "yes, Socrates." In the *Phaedo,* on the other hand, he encourages and even stimulates extremely powerful objections to his position. In the *Apology,* he follows the conventional lines of a rhetorical lecture (besides the cross-examination of Meletus). In the *Phaedrus* he interposes an inspirational lecture on love. Even in the same dialogue (*Gorgias*) in which he asks his interlocutor to confine himself to short statements, he himself is soon giving fairly lengthy ones. Thus, at the purely formal level, the only reasonable position is an eclectic one.

The difficulty with the antiauthoritarian methodology is that it tends to obscure weaknesses in present classroom methods by encouraging a single view of them. Thus, Rossman, for whom the university classroom today is the mold of the "authority complex" in American life, finds that "teaching, in higher education is generally taken to mean a particular way of conveying information that is already known."[6] This statement has the advantage that it is attending to the actual process of communication rather than only to the relations of the persons. But the grave disadvantage is the extent to which it equates very diverse processes. The notion that even the routine introductory physics or mathematics courses at the university level consist of information transmission is misleading, for that notion of them allows us to equate scientific ideas with inert facts. To follow a mechanically deductive proof of a theorem of the sort illustrated in Chapter Eight is one sort of mental operation; to memorize tables of propositions or elements that have little more rationale than the alphabet is quite another; to equate them blurs

[6] Rossman, *loc. cit.,* p. 25.

151

the problem of teaching. Many students do of course complain that the science and math courses that "turned them off" did so because the courses only presented material for rote memorization. When too many students are turned off, something is wrong, but the students' analysis of it may not be the correct one. The difference between being turned off by a supposed chain of reasoning and by a collection of facts is one they ignore in favor of regarding both as information transmission from authority. Thus, they decide that the remedy lies in eliminating "transmission" and giving status to students' thoughts on the question. However, the real problem may be that there are missing links between steps in the instructor's argument. The instructor is used to telescoping such steps and is not sensitive to their omission. In such a situation, the need is not to detach an argument from an authority figure but simply to give the reasoning explicit logical continuity.

The "information-transmission" stereotype also leads to the view that a difficulty with the present classroom method is that it isolates subjects from matters of larger significance. What is needed to counteract this fragmentation, according to this criticism, is to bring into interplay a diversity of points of view so that a larger synthesis can be achieved. Hence, there is a call for free discussion among equals. The reasoning seems to be that the expert's narrowness shows authoritarian rigidity. We would argue that the opposite is the case: that the impression of authoritarianism is more likely to be given when faculty fail to stay within their proper boundaries or to make clear what those boundaries are. When a teacher implicitly offers his position as unrestricted truth or allows his problem to be taken as embodying the whole truth, he is obscuring the inherent piecemeal character of his subject. In Chapter Eight, we dealt with a Euclidean idea in order to show how such an idea is tied to its particular framework of assumptions and how an awareness of this framework should prevent its partisans from claiming it to be the one true picture of space. Indeed, the pictures it does provide are significant mainly when seen within the boundaries the frame sets. When such limitations are made explicit, then teaching comes closer to a specific truth and has a built-in guard against the most danger-

Teaching Methods

ous kind of authoritarianism—that of men or groups who think they have, or are unambiguously on the road to, truth itself.

METHOD

In the antiauthoritarian view, the present classroom method of simply presenting subject matter leaves the student passive and thus gives evidence of the need for innovative methods that engage him. In order to engage the student, the subject matter must be intellectually alive. In this context, we think it important that university courses employ a range of the diverse methods that go into developing an idea. In the context of autonomous ideas, any given method can be adapted to the idea it is structuring and developing. For example, discovery occurs in watching a play and in writing one, in resolving some practical dilemmas and in solving a scientific problem; the form of discovery will likely be different in each case. Such variation is one source of an idea's vitality or freshness. Our earlier elaborations of autonomous ideas in diverse areas are thus no less illustrations of method, or psychological process, than of content.

Because of its complexity and diversity, we cannot here offer a schematism of methods, but we can note a major source of them: namely, the diversity of books and articles on subjects studied in a course or curriculum. We speak sometimes as if the people present in the educational process are the one teacher and the students: books well selected and well diversified are men, as Milton said, and often are the best teachers in a course or the best safeguards against rigidity. To point out the virtues of books in a book on education in the university is simpleminded, but that we should need to do so is a sign of a voiceless part of the university today. The reason for the need is perhaps evident in the theme of this chapter: that for a university, method is not a matter of how people interact, but of how they interact in and through ideas.

LEARNING AND JUDGMENT

A prevailing student complaint today about current methods that interfere with learning is the use of grades and the grading process. The professor grades the student and wields an ultimate authority in so doing. The very process reinforces the notion of authority in its most external and meaningless sense. All the ills of the system seem to reside in just this process. The student must undergo the process of having his performance graded; he cannot function freely in a purely learning process; he is compelled to learn and hand back to the teacher what the teacher gave him, or he will suffer the consequences of bad grades. The whole process of study and learning is thus degraded to a simple mechanical stimulus-response situation.

It has been argued that a university as a resource of knowledge should function like a public library. It should be open to all to take whatever they are interested in and can absorb, as much or as little as they like, as long or as short a time as they like, and then go their own way. There should be no admissions problems, nor any grading processes. Each student picks up what is appropriate for him and then uses it in his life as he wishes. Milton's remarks about good books are quite appropriate for this ideal. And for young geniuses and older persons who have attained the ability of intellectual self-criticism that this process assumes, this is a perfectly appropriate kind of educational process. Probably such process obtained in Plato's Academy and Aristotle's Lyceum. Only those interested in the problems being pursued participated in the processes of learning and searching for new knowledge; they were, in effect, self-selected. This process is visible in special institutions of higher learning where the participants are those already recognized as having attained the abilities of self-criticism. But this situation is hardly typical for the mass of those in our undergraduate university system today. Rather, the university is the place where the fires of critical self-directed learning should be lit for some, but where the search for such illumination is still going on for many others.

There is nothing sacred about any set of grading symbols from A to F or 0 to 100. Prolonged arguments in various student-faculty committees have been devoted to the significance of letter grades and their possible replacement by a simple Pass/Fail marking in some courses. Every process inevitably must provide for the discrimination of those who are better in given areas and those who are being urged to go elsewhere. Encouragement and discouragement are facts of life that guide all men into channels where their talents can best be developed and employed.

There are, of course, difficulties in all guidance systems. Yet, as in most human activities, achievement eventually is recognized, and rewards and responsibilities are generally distributed in accord with achievement. In a most direct way, this is true in university activity. Those who excel and enjoy the activity receive immediately the intrinsic rewards inherent in the activity itself. The external signs, however devised and executed, are ultimately mere shorthand devices that aid the movement of such self-selected persons from place to place and position to position as they build cumulatively their own abilities for further activities.

Recognizing the facts of life on this problem does not equate being "realistic" in the sense of accepting necessary evils and unwholesome motivations. Diverse selection processes are as prominent in utopia as in actuality. In plans as different as Plato's *Republic* and Skinner's *Walden II* regulative judgments remain, although attention is given to means of assuring their right use by judge and judged alike. The dignity and ego of students will be sustained by altering social misjudgments of the function and meaning of grades, not by eliminating grades. Thus, the problem rests in the social context and the quality of university life itself. It is the essence of this quality, not the secondary instruments employed in it, to which this book has been devoted and to which thought about the university should return.

Religion

❦ 13 ❦

The commonplace expression "Man does not live by bread alone" perhaps summarizes one aspect of the great feelings of discontent among young people today. The material satisfactions are found to be essentially empty, as they most certainly are when taken as an end in themselves. This truism was known long ago by many perceptive people, but today, with widespread affluence in our culture, there is greater recognition of this basic truth. The flower children have rediscovered it and attempted to remove themselves from the pressures and necessities upon which our economic and political system operates. Even the revolutionaries have been compelled to restate the grounds for revolution from the class consciousness of the poor against the rich (as developed by Marx) to the self-consciousness of those seeking freedom from the enslavement of the system (as stated by Marcuse).

Part of the students' search for identity is an attempt to establish a connection of themselves with their picture of the total universe encompassing them. Not living "by bread alone" clearly expresses the human consciousness that goes beyond individual needs to a total perspective by which each person can orient himself to the world as he experiences it. Usually, individuals obtain a set of beliefs from their family, the tribe, or the nation. Plato recognized the necessity for a religious education in his ideal state as a means of unifying the society around a simple set of beliefs about the world as a whole. For him, this education was truly primary, for it came in the stories told children prior to their readiness for a gymnastic education. This kind of education was a simple indoctrination in the basic concept that the gods had made all good things in the world. Apparently this would produce a sense of security in the total world picture as a basis for the individual's confidence that his actions ultimately have beneficial results. Indeed, studies have shown that the most stable and productive persons are produced in societies in which the society's need for each individual is made clear and his place in it is most assured (for example, Bettelheim's study on an Israeli kibbutz). For Plato, this most elementary education pointed the children in the right direction for what was ultimately to be the fullest possible intellectual development.

Perhaps the lukewarm and purely social function of religion in their parents' generation led to such ideological permissiveness in the raising of present university students that their religious training has indeed lost all meaning for them. Some have returned to more orthodox practices than those followed by their parents; others have rejected completely the empty religious orientation of their families and sought elsewhere for a more meaningful experience. Students have identified themselves as "formerly Jewish" or "formerly Catholic" as they embrace various forms of Buddhism that have grasped their interest. The search among university students for direct, ultimately meaningful experience is widespread. In large numbers, they subscribe to courses on myth, mysticism, philosophy of religion, Oriental philosophy, existentialism, and metaphysics. Lectures given on Japanese magical practices draw large audiences, while interesting lectures on recent scientific discoveries by experts (even the discoverers themselves) are relatively poorly attended.

A striking example of this pervasive student interest occurred in the middle of the 1969 fall semester at Stony Brook, when two panel discussions were held in a residential college on two Monday evenings two weeks apart. Popular professors from anthropology, English, and philosophy departments spoke on the first topic of "Myth" while equally popular men from physics, history of science, and philosophy spoke on the second topic of "Scientific Revolutions." On the first occasion, the college lounge overflowed with students eagerly interested in pursuing the topic; on the second occasion, a few faculty members attended, and one or two students drifted in and out during the discussion.

The Voiceless University

It seems reasonable to conclude that students seek the significance of mystical experiences, of occult sciences, and of myth as expressions of fundamental human feelings, knowledge, and insight. But some persons will be tempted to minimize the significance of these facts by maintaining that our students today are pursuing the easy subjects, the ones most readily involving their feelings and most directly experienceable. These persons point to the larger proportion of high school graduates who enter universities, believing that this increase has lowered the general ability of the "average" student; it is suggested that these students undertake the less demanding work in order to be able to get through the university. There may be a grain of truth in this type of argument, but it is also true that many students with unquestionable ability also have similar interests. And further, among the best students we have ever encountered are individuals who have had deeply moving religious experiences. We would not therefore draw a line between good students and those seeking satisfaction of this basic human impulse.

The discontent associated with the search for satisfaction of this impulse is often telescoped with other particular grievances or with some general revolutionary search for an overall immediate solution to our social problems. Yet this source of discontent deserves a separate examination to determine what place religion should have in higher education.

First, it should be noted that religion has long had a recognized place in most institutions of higher education. Even if we ignore the colleges supported and run by religious institutions, where a common set of beliefs is assumed to exist among the students, we find that in large universities, public and private (some formerly established by specific religious groups), account is taken of religion as a pervasive element in human life. There are psychological, sociological, historical, philosophical, and literary studies and accounts of religious experiences and institutions. For example, studies in comparative religions from a variety of perspectives, literary interpretations of myths in various cultures, religious expressions in various poems and prose compositions, philosophical reflection on the religious experience (William James), sociological studies of various religious institutions, and philosophical examinations of the various proofs of God's existence and criticisms of such proofs have long been parts of university curricula. Thus, in terms of understanding religion in human culture on the one hand and of examining comparative and systematic grounds for religious truth claims on the other, there is already much available in most university curricula.

In addition, many universities grant credit toward graduation for a limited number of courses taken in associated religious foundations, such courses being in the history and doctrine of the particular religions. Such outside work is apparently considered acceptable to satisfy the felt need for reinforcing the specific commitments of adherents to various religious beliefs. Perhaps this opportunity fills in the gap between studies judged central to a university and the needs that go beyond the province of a university discipline.

Clearly, in times of great social disorder and/or individual stress, individuals rediscover for themselves the religious grounds upon which to reorient their thoughts and lives. Certainly the search for intellectual and practical security is the burden of each individual as he organizes his ideas and life. The account of Augustine and others testifies to this search. For Augustine, the emptiness of all human knowledge and the discovery that all he formerly valued was valueless led ultimately to a psychic revolution—individualized acts of intuition, a conversion to an ultimate source of truth and value. But the unique character of such an experience attests to the fact that evoking such experiences can in no way be a part of a university curriculum.

Yet this basic human impulse does lead students (as it did Augustine) to believe that the successful piecemeal treatment of problems of knowledge and action is unsatisfactory. Educational successes have been achieved by such piecemeal processes, but these processes apparently are contrary to the direct attachment of an individual with a wholistic view of the universe. Whitehead has indicated the incompleteness of the piecemeal tactic taken alone:

159

The Voiceless University

"The essence of education is that it be religious."
"Pray, what is religious education?"
"A religious education is an education which inculcates duty and reverence. Duty arises from our potential control over the course of events. Where attainable knowledge could have changed the issue, ignorance has the guilt of the vice. And the foundation of reverence is this perception, that the present holds within itself the complete sum of existence, backwards and forwards, that whole amplitude of time, which is eternity."[1]

Thus, both in the realm of action and of knowledge, some awareness of the involvement of any part with the whole in which it exists is essential to satisfy the virtues of duty and reverence. In any bit or part, there is involved the totality of all that is; the fragment is a fragment of the whole, dimly felt and understood. Thus, we are presented with the obligation to act on and to understand any portion as reaching beyond the devices we use to delimit it for our action and understanding. This sense of the whole is not a point of focus by means of which one attains ultimate security in an insecure world, but it is a framework implicit in all we do and think.

Kant has indicated the ever-present character of man's perspective of the totality of things in two quite different ways. He also indicates the sources of value of these two ways and the inherent dangers in leaping to final conclusions about the totality without inquiry and reason:

Two things fill the mind with ever new and increasing admiration and awe, the oftener and the more steadily we reflect on them: the starry heavens above and the moral law within. *I have not to search for them and conjecture them as though they were veiled in darkness or were in the transcendent region beyond my horizon; I see them before me and connect them directly with the consciousness of my existence. The former begins from the place I occupy in the external world of sense, and enlarges my connexion therein to an unbounded*

---

[1] A. N. Whitehead, "The Aims of Education," in *The Aims of Education* (New York: The New American Library, 1948), pp. 25–26.

extent with worlds upon worlds and systems of systems, and more-over into limitless times of their periodic motion, its beginning and continuance. The second begins from my invisible self, my personality, and exhibits me in a world which has true infinity, but which is traceable only by the understanding, and with which I discern that I am not in a merely contingent but in a universal and necessary connexion, as I am also thereby with all those visible worlds. The former view of a countless multitude of worlds annihilates, as it were, my importance as an animal creature, *which after it has been a short time provided with vital power, one knows not how, must again give back the matter of which it was formed to the planet it inhabits (a mere speck in the universe). The second, on the contrary, infinitely elevates my worth as an* intelligence *by my personality, in which the moral law reveals to me a life independent on animality and even on the whole sensible world—at least so far as may be inferred from the destination assigned to my existence by this law, a destination not restricted to conditions and limits of this life, but reaching into the infinite. But though admiration and respect may excite to inquiry, they cannot supply the want of it. What, then, is to be done in order to enter on this in a useful manner and one adapted to the loftiness of the subject? Examples may serve in this as a warning, and also for imitation. The contemplation of the world began from the noblest spectacle that the human senses present to us, and that our understanding can bear to follow in their vast reach; and it ended—in astrology. Morality began with the noblest attribute of human nature, the development and cultivation of which give a prospect of infinite utility; and ended—in fanaticism or superstition.*[2]

At this point in his argument, Kant indicated the great success that reason has had in replacing astrology by Newtonian celestial mechanics. He suggests by analogy that the moral judgments of reason, when analyzed into their elementary conceptions—that is, when separated into empirical and rational elements—can

[2] E. Kant, *Critique of Practical Reason,* tr. Abbot (New York: Longmans, Green & Co., Ltd., 1948), pp. 260–261.

achieve a similar success and certainty, thereby avoiding the errors of crude untrained judgment and the extravagances of genius.

Whitehead and Kant have thus taken account of this basic human impulse in different ways; but each emphasizes the necessity for inquiry and reason in grasping the significance of this ultimate human perspective. Each might also recognize that the university cannot and should not attempt to present some ultimate insight satisfying to the students. On the contrary, it should present the diversity of man's attempt to come to grips with such felt needs, the difficulties involved in satisfying such needs despite the genuineness of the need itself. If the university teaches of these attempts, it will have provided the grounds for each to shape his own ideas and style of life.

Since the beginnings of Western civilization, religious institutions as well as universities have been accused of stifling the true human spirit with ritual, routine laws, and ceremonies. On the other side, established religions and universities have warned against the fanatic and the false enthusiasm of the misguided. In an obvious sense, the truly religious person is not confined to any particular set of beliefs. And besides the unique nobility of character that each such person reveals, it also is perhaps true that persons having had such experiences can be identified generally by a simple rule of thumb: they feel able to communicate with certitude their experiences in exactly inverse proportion to the depth of the experience. Such a rule of thumb, along with the opportunities offered in a university for examining the ways in which thinkers such as Whitehead and Kant have expressed their insights into this side of human nature, may make us somewhat wary of the variety of directions in which expression is now being given by many of our youth today to this fundamental human impulse.

We should certainly not discount the psychological satisfactions that students receive from chanting magical Japanese words or from the myths of Vedic writings or from the negative arguments of idealistic Oriental philosophies. The appeal of the foreign and exotic is great as compared with the more familiar magical practices, myths, and idealistic arguments in Western traditions. Indeed, so powerful is the appeal that students demand that batteries of courses be offered "in" such approaches to provide the relevant experiences; this request often receives sympathetic hearing in today's supply-and-demand curricular market. We already have argued the reasons that the university classroom cannot be made responsible for actually infusing the authentic, any more than the inauthentic, religious experience. But the demand does highlight the fact that the university does have a curricular responsibility in this new region of interest; it has the double obligation to examine rigorously the magic, myth, and idealistic arguments, and to make probing comparisons between the familiar and exotic traditions. The distinction between personal enthusiasms and profound religious experiences must be made—especially as we can now produce apparently similar feelings nearly at will by using one of a large number of diverse "mind-expanding" drugs. This very fact has allowed cynics to devalue all accounts of profound religious experiences as merely specific chemical interactions, despite the fact that most humans in one way or another have comprehensive perspectives of the world as a basis for orienting themselves in life.

Enduring Object

 FIVE

This concluding part returns to the original question of the role of the university in a world of change today but treats it in terms of principles of the university. These principles put the focus on what is constant in university activity and on its enduring value through historical change (Chapter Fourteen). Finally (Chapter Fifteen), the present cultural and political situation is assessed for possible dangers to the university and for signs of support among those who are aware of the value of the university.

University
and
Change

☙ 14 ☙

The present marks the climax of a philosophical climate, which has been building up since Darwin, in which change is crucial to life and the world. Pragmatism, creative evolution, instrumentalism, positivism, operationalism, existentialism—nearly all the major movements in their simpler versions emphasize their break from fixed forms. In similarly reductive versions, all other disciplines have found their respective Linnaeus to reject. Art is a good barometer here; instead of a new form to replace the novel, we get the antinovel with its antihero. Similarly, novelty becomes a supposedly ultimate value in its own right when painting sets up the "tradition of the new." Change is seen no longer as the means to a desired end, but as an end in itself; for life is change.

This background generates and supports the importunate call for change in the university (or the counterpleas that the university hold fast). New theories have appeared that build their explanations of the university's ills and their proposals for remedy on this concept. But obviously there must be intelligible inquiries into factual complexes in order to articulate the options and determine the direction of change; and even the choice of direction, difficult as it is, leaves open additional problems of stability, or at least continuity. In neglecting such considerations, the new theorists seem to us to be following the fashion rather than coming to grips with the substantial problems.

As illustration, let us examine two theories that contain representative arguments of what we regard as "fashionable"; we call them the developmental educational theory and the neohumanist theory. We will indicate first some of the main tenets of each, then their common origin in the focus on change, and finally what we take to be their deficiencies.

One of the most widely read accounts of the developmental educational theory is found in *The Student in Higher Education,* published by The Hazen Foundation. The argument of this document emphasizes the process of growth of university students from adolescence to early adulthood. It finds that the needs of the student during this period are personal identity and intimacy. It emphasizes the necessity to educate the *whole* human being—to take into account the affective nature of man as well as the intellectual. It argues the inappropriateness and abstractness of a purely intellectual education, particularly at a period when the emotional and experiential side of man's nature is undergoing marked development. The report concludes with various recommendations for building a new life for students, based to a large extent on the specific recommendation that "the power of the faculty over undergraduate education be greatly reduced."[1]

The neohumanist theory emphasizes not the genetic or developmental aspects of the student, but his search for dignity in a technologically dominated world of confused values. The student is seeking to reconstitute the individual humanistic sense of worth lost in our mass culture in which individuals are cogs in a vast machine. The focus here is upon the ultimate human needs that must be satisfied. The disruptions of the universities are essentially expressions of the students' recognition and rejection of the mass educational system in which they lose their individuality. The humanist decries the values of the affluent society as empty, materialistic, and

[1] *The Student in Higher Education* (New Haven, Conn.: The Hazen Foundation, 1968), p. 62.

167

meaningless. The waste of the economy, the destruction of natural beauty, the pollution of our environment are all indications of the false values of the system that produces them. The opposition between the system of the Establishment and the uniqueness of the individual seeking simple values lies at the root of the humanist search for a revolution in values to reconstitute our lives.

There is much in common between the developmental and the humanist theories. Although the one is oriented toward the genetic and the other toward ultimate human ends, they both use a basic split between the mechanical, technological, and scientific system on the one hand and the human, organic, unique experiential values on the other. One of the characteristic ways in which philosophies make the break from fixed forms is by setting up authentic human action and self-expression as the source and arbiter of values, and even of facts. Action and expression are characterized essentially by process and movement and so are guarantees against fixity of any sort.

The difficulty with these theories is not that they wish to attend to action and experience, but that they tend to take these factors as more or less sufficient criteria of what is good or bad in education. Theory is thus assimilated to—often simply reduced to—the fashion. In their worst form, the theories deal with a variety of problems simply by finding the basic good/bad split mirrored variously—for example, personal/computerized, emotive/intellectual, liberal/professional, end/means, men/machines, love/war. These simplistic splits, of course, do not do justice to the values and potentialities now built into our educational system.

In particular, the developmentalist, in emphasizing that learning must be meaningful to the student personally, seems to ignore the fact that even professional learning is far more than mere acquisition of information; it generates its own excitement and joy in understanding what was not understood before, and it is therefore novel. Thus, the developmentalist seems to overlook the possibility that intellectual insight may be the epitome of meaningful experience and pleasure for all men—although different men can achieve such experiences at different levels and at different times in their lives.

The developmentalist focuses rather on the kind of pleasure in the learning experience that derives from the nondisciplined or only quasi-intellectual interests of the young. Although admitting that sufficient evidence about these matters is not yet available, the developmentalist recommends, for example, that the first year of university work be an "orientation to learning," because the student is interested primarily in globular ideas and large theories rather than precise ideas about limited areas. We, too, believe that these predisciplinary experiences with ideas—what Whitehead calls the "romance" of ideas and what Plato called their music—are essential. But these experiences are preparatory in ways the developmentalist seems to neglect. First, the shift from them to disciplined learning is from one level of pleasure to another (and high school should put the student at least on the verge of the second level). Second, the stages are also intellectually connected, the first a lead-in to the second, so that the developmentalist's assumption that the professional orientation should be barred from the education of freshmen seems to construct an unnecessary and dangerous schism. Indeed, the noted new texts that have been developed even for the high school level by professionals in biology, mathematics, and other areas result from bridging that schism.

The neohumanist, however, emphasizes the values of immediate experience as more emotionally significant than the dryness of intellectual and scientific orientations. It is easy to reject the bad when considered in this abstract way. But in so doing, one neglects two critical features: the interwoven network of values and the process of value transmission.

In the context of the first feature, we value pollution-free air and private units of transportation, but this combination is not available to us today. An indefinite number of other values make up a network of values with many similar incompatibilities. Such incompatibilities occasion the recognition of problems and the search for solutions. Industry seeks pollution-free automobiles, and others seek solutions to other recognized incompatibilities. Universities have a key role in this entire process, for they are technological and intellectual resources for seeking solutions. Further, in making us aware of the network of value, the university can reveal the inherent ties of immediate, felt values with the discursive structure of value— contrary to the new theorist's view that these two are incompatible.

Second, even the transmission of value involves its transformation and so becomes a revaluation. New values are not merely those being sought in some distant future; they are found in the classroom itself, in that each class period constitutes a novel situation. Any subject matter involves a working over of old values under new contexts or circumstances, so that new values emerge in the teaching-learning processes. The irony is that while new theorists go far afield in search of sources of new-felt values, the university in its present structure provides means and conditions for constructing some of them ourselves—although admittedly these possibilities will not be actualized when professor and student are unaware of them.

Perhaps attention should also be given to a third sort of theory, which involves another, more subtle kind of simplification generated by the fashion for change. This simplification appears in sophisticated versions of social radicalism that see in the university a source of the sociophilosophic ideas which, by making men active rather than docile, will bring about the desired changes. Christopher Lasch and Eugene Genovese argue this view, and Charles Reich argues that our youth is leading us to such a new light. What interests us is that they conclude with a call for "a new cultural synthesis" as the overall objective. But the leap from the need for change to the need for a "synthesis," or new "consciousness," is tremendous. The need might be instead for an understanding of the pragmatic inappropriateness and possible intellectual weakness of "a new cultural synthesis, based on the rationalist tradition,"[2] and

[2] Christopher Lasch and Eugene Genovese, "The Education and the University We Need Now," *New York Review of Books,* October 9, 1969, p. 27.

the dangerous illusion of wisdom in an inchoate "Consciousness III," rooted in simple clothes and basic rhythms.[3]

Lest our criticism of the prevailing fashion be misunderstood, we should add here the positive aspect of our view toward it. Shifts in fashion can be the occasion for significant advances in philosophy and other disciplines (as suggested by the title of Suzanne Langer's *Philosophy in a New Key*). The same possibility applies to theories of education. The danger comes when the new key is blown up into monolithic and simplistic reductions of a complex problem. How we would develop a new key is based on two assumptions that we have made evident a number of times. They are (1) that there is *no* one "real" answer; there are different problems requiring different, often isolable, piecemeal analyses and approaches, and (2) that the focus on change should serve as *a way into,* not an abandonment of, the articulation of useful structures and continuities, and as a way into rather than a turning away from varied uses of the intellectual.

Our position is easily illustrated. Let us take imaginative literature and drama as a piecemeal problem. The use of the fashion can lead to significant advances in many ways, of which we indicate three here. First, even without a predisposition to reject traditional literary forms, we can test those forms for the extent to which they can be incorporated in the new modes of life introduced by technological and other changes.

Second, the orientation to experience and process has opened up the possibility of seeing in the most ordinary encounters in life, dramatic significances that the Greeks, for example, could achieve only with remote and eminent figures clashing in the political arena. This imaginative reconstruction of the processes of experience is not an unstructured neorealism, but rather it can become in the hands of the best authors an excitingly patterned exhibition of the structures and rhythms of supposedly trivial processes. Those

[3] Charles Reich, *The Greening of America* (New York: Random House, 1970).

persons who would cite Eric Kahler and others to lament the "disintegration of form" should bear in mind the form and structure that the new fashion can cause to be discovered in unsuspected places—even the inconsequential talk in the home of Joyce or Pinter. The result can be an enrichment of every man's view of his own life and experience.

Third, even the new passion for novelty can be most richly exploited on our two tenets. Meaningful novelty, experience as such, cannot exist in abstraction; it is only novel in context. We cannot be astonished by something if we are not aware of it as different from what is in some manner ordinary. In its experiential dimension, novelty is valued as getting out of a rut or a routine. Now literature can achieve this novelty by presenting recognizable experiences in an unfamiliar light; in time, the presentation can become a familiar artistic view from which another art work can in turn deviate. For an artist to be inventive and creatively deviant, he must be intensely sensitive to norms; and these norms can remain implicit and unrecognized until he becomes sensitive to opportunities for change and can make them overt. Finally, the basis for the unexpected can be laid by establishing patterns within the work and then breaking them before the work's end. (This is how the Greeks did it.)

The general point we are making—that for art to produce novelty, it must have structure and meaning—can be seen by considering the efforts made to ignore this rule. At first ordinary conventions supply enough material to highlight the artist's other acts or thoughts as unconventional. But as no further structures or meanings are built, there has to be a straining for strangeness. Ultimately, such works or happenings, instead of generating the background for astonishment, degenerate into a sequence of discontinuities. The sense of novelty is achieved by insisting that there be no connection between any two elements in a series. Here we *are* in danger of the disintegration of form, not because of attention to change, but because change itself has been reduced to physical motion or otherwise impoverished.

Advances made through considering the use of change as a key are similarly possible, and often neglected, in all areas. In the

172

mass media, for example, actionally effective communication tends today to be reduced to devices of attention getting. The alternative is to try at least to broaden common understanding so that a new idea rather than a melee will attract attention. At the other extreme, in the area of the sciences, it is evident that a far-reaching discovery could not be recognized as such except against the background of the body of knowledge it illuminates and expands.

CHANGE IN THE UNIVERSITY

We do not hold with a general metaphysical doctrine that holds that all reality is change—a doctrine that is some 2300 years old—nor do we go with the recent fashion that modern society is especially marked by pure instability and rapid transitions. Charges are made that basic changes have taken place that our educational system has not properly taken into account and that, therefore, there is an unbridgeable chasm between the present state of society and the old-fashioned, worn-out educational institutions. This recent fashion has appeared to us to overemphasize current states of mind, to project them into a view about our current educational problems, and to offer no principles for judging the kinds and quantity of changes needed in university education today.

The history of educational theory and practice, as found in Plato and Aristotle, the Romans, medieval thought, the Renaissance, and on through to the twentieth century, is full of innovators pressing hard for new ideas and for revolutions in educational theory and practice. In the late nineteenth century, Darwin's discoveries sparked a revolution in education as scientists fought to gain for the new science its rightful place in the educational scheme. The older cultural ideas—sometimes bound up with prevailing theology—resisted the impact of the new young scientific truth-tellers. Yet those new ideas clearly changed the educational scheme and have produced university curricula of such diversity as to offer a vast number of alternatives to students today. Similar revolts, on a smaller scale, recur again and again. The theory and practice of education are full of innovation and revolution. Change is so constant that one wonders if the cry for change can ever be innovative.

173

The Voiceless University

At a less general level, continual changes are made as new experimental courses are added and older courses and methods of organizing subject matters are dropped. These changes reflect the general advance of knowledge as new, promising fields of study are opened up by researchers pursuing their inquiries. Usually, addition of new courses at an upper level in a given subject matter is an easy matter, whereas a more fundamental change in general outlook in a given discipline, requiring the restructuring of a total curriculum, involves a time lag.

Campus unrest can hardly be traced to the kind of changes treated here, which are internal—that is, the initiating agency is university faculty, and the process is a normal extension of university activities. Even the time lag in achieving the restructuring of a total departmental curriculum is seldom apparent to students majoring in the department, let alone a ground for action on a campuswide basis for major structural changes in the whole university.

There are also external forces for change to be considered. Obviously, universities are social institutions that depend upon the support of the society of which they are a part for their continued existence and well-being. Clearly, also, various social forces external to universities have affected them at various times in the course of Western history. Political authorities have exercised control: the Roman Republic at one period outlawed foreigners teaching in Rome, and after Christianization, the Roman Empire closed the ancient academies started by Plato, Aristotle, and others. Upon other occasions religious forces have exercised power over university activities, such as the suppression of Galileo's teachings or the religious censure of nonorthodox books. Such regressive forces have serious damaging effects at given times and places, yet fortunately they appear to have no lasting effect upon the autonomous university activity, which has not been diverted from its path since the beginnings of Western intellectual history some 2500 years ago.

It is undeniable that a massive catastrophe could bring the university to an end. But in this event, the human race or even all life on earth could probably disappear. In a period when humans did not possess the power of self-destruction, Gibbon[4] reflected on the breakdown of civilization in the Western empire and the possibilities of such a breakdown recurring. He concluded that even if all the major institutions were destroyed, at least the primitive arts like agriculture, metal working, and weaving would survive, preventing man from descending into pure savagery and forming the base for rebuilding civilization. However one interprets this period of the so-called Dark Ages (and some scholars now find evidence of considerable cultural activity during this period), the basic arts of discourse, writing, and critical argument survived. And new institutions of higher learning evolved as general political stability was reestablished in the area.

Certainly, there have been periods of relative intellectual quiescence during the past twenty-five centuries as compared with other periods of great creativity and advance. Whitehead notes this fact about the cycles of productivity in the history of mathematics. Perhaps political disturbances could account for some of these inactive periods; however, most of the periods of quiescence may have resulted from the fact that fewer men of great genius became involved in intellectual activity.

Finally, at any given period, parts of civilized society may restrict areas of free discourse within their national boundaries—an action that clearly damages those nations. However, even in such restrictive societies, freedoms are allowed in other areas, and the boundaries of the restricted areas are probed both from within and from without the nation. In some cases, restrictions are ultimately abandoned—for example, the recent Lysenkoan restrictions on biological theory in Russia.

Thus, despite local disturbances and minor modifications due to local conditions and pressures, the core of university activity has been essentially untouched by external forces. One might argue that this human activity is essentially untouchable by outside forces and

[4] Edward Gibbon, *The Decline and Fall of the Roman Empire* (New York: The Modern Library), Vol. II, pp. 90–98.

175

that such forces ultimately retract after having infringed upon this basic activity.

But some may feel that a different source of change is welling up within our universities that must undergo vast restructuring. It should be remembered, however, that other waves of romanticisms have swept through Western culture, and the university activity has survived. New ideas can enliven and energize our educational system, even as they undergo scrutiny to determine their value for incorporation within a university curricula. Ultimately, the standards within the university determine the value and survivability of ideas for university adoption. In this sense, although additions and modifications may be made to an ongoing curricula, the basic structure and activity in the university remains self-determining.

UNIVERSITY AS SOURCE OF SOCIAL CHANGE

In addition to being criticized for its rigidities in structure, curriculum, and procedures, the university also is viewed as a key source of change outside itself. In this final section, we wish to consider it in this role by regrouping points made in preceding parts of the book. The most striking changes the university generates, and those most visible to the public, are scientific and technological changes based on intellectually responsible analyses of current developments. Similarly, in cultural activities external to the university, its functions are expanding rapidly. The ties between professionals in the universities and advances in literature, theater, and art are multiplying.

So extensive is the university's role in external change that we benefit from noting its limitations. First, the university is not the seat of the wisdom the public sometimes expects from it (when not in an anti-egghead mood). The expectation that it is such a center is nourished by some of the professional humanists, social theorists, and scientists who in various ways present themselves as wise men. They had their counterparts in the poets, politicians, and artisans of ancient Athens, whom Socrates questioned in his search for a wise man. He found that each man, indeed, did have some knowledge or other expertise of value, but that in each case this limited accomplishment was thought by its possessor to be the key to all problems. Such false claims to wisdom are particularly damaging when they seem to discredit the piecemeal character of discplined inquiry. The university can have a constructive effect when its professionals are sensitive to their limitations; otherwise they provide some ground for the foolish anti-egghead contempt.

To this intellectual limitation on the university's role in change we must add a sociopolitical one. Remembering Whitehead's argument on the influence of ideas, members of the university easily conceive it as the hinge of history. It is the hinge, no doubt, from the standpoint of the long-run workings of ideas in society. But those workings are mediated through many institutions, of which the university is but one. Even in terms of long-run effect, the church and the family can as well see themselves at the crux of the future.

Finally, we note a limitation on the university's role that follows from the nature of academic freedom. At its core, this freedom is not a gift from political authority but is inherent in intellectual activity itself, for such activity assumes that truth and falsity are not politically determinable. It is not that they ought not to be so decided, but that they cannot be. However, for the same reason, the intellectual activities of the university can have no political status; the university is ideally a bearer of truth, not of power. We have here drawn the distinction between the academic and the political starkly and abstractly, but in practice academic freedom must carry the right of political activity, and conversely, the needs of society affect the university's functions. However, these necessary and complex relations must nonetheless be worked out only in conformity with the abstract distinction drawn above—that intellectual activities and political activities are each autonomous in their spheres. Society curtails or expands public university budgets, and faculty members exert their due influence as participating citizens in political affairs. But recognition of the separation of the autonomous spheres puts strong brakes on society's claims and assures that in the university's classrooms and laboratories, findings are based on proof alone. This "limitation," like the others, obviously is not a shortcoming, but instead a boundary within which the university

177

has autonomy and can make the internal advances that can in turn have widening external effects.

Our concern so far in this section has been the influence the university exerts through the professionals who lead its intellectual activity. A still more pervasive influence takes shape in and through the alumni, who are making up an ever higher percentage of the population. Earlier parts of our study examined some features of university education in terms of this later external role: the bases for alumni's carrying on various activities independently of a professor were examined in Chapter Two; the models university life provides for participation in various kinds of community were discussed in Three; sociopolitical relevance in Four; and religious questions in Thirteen. But we wish here finally, to reraise the question others prefer to begin with: how does the student's diverse experience in the university years hang together? Should this experience not provide a unified outlook, since without one, no matter how rigorous the specific items of acquired knowledge, the person is adrift? We will not try here to rejustify our claim that an overarching wisdom is not directly teachable. Nor are we here discussing religious belief. Rather we are raising the question of the general effect on the student of his years of disciplined inquiry in the university. The claim we made in Chapter Two was that "in the stimulation provided by disciplined inquiry lies as good a chance as there is for awakening wisdom indirectly." While these inquiries add to the individual's knowledge of the particular subject, at the same time they add to his repeatable experience in confronting and coping with new situations. All phases of life in a university community broaden this experience. There should develop from it over time not a system of knowledge from which to deduce judgments and choices but habits of mind of the sort that are tied to and stimulate the uses of reason. The student does not get a unified picture of the world from this source, it is true, but he does have a stable disposition to approach problems and situations as responsive to reason.

This approach cannot guarantee subsequent success, particularly not on the many important issues that remain matters of opinion. Success in these cases depends on insight and intuitive perception of the best opinion in the circumstances.

So far as there can be training for such perception, the university years are of the greatest value. That disciplined, systematic inquiries should have value for "nonscientizable" opinion is remarkable but not surprising. In becoming trained to work out, step by step, the structure of a problem and its solutions in course after course, the mind multiplies its encounters with rational solutions; there should accordingly develop a gradual improvement in the capacity for immediate recognition of the most reasonable opinion in variable situations. In sum, other things being equal, right opinion on the choices and chances of life for the individual and society tends to come to the disciplined mind. That the formation and encouragement of such minds is a primary end of the university has been the theme of this book.

In general then, we have attempted to provide a new perspective on the essential structure of university education as it has been operative in our culture for over two thousand years. In one sense, we have merely examined a formal structure that is essentially unchanged. Yet novelty invariably enters as the university reasserts its role in terms of its context of the moment. Seeing this novelty in the total context of the university's stability opens up a new basis for reanalyzing our present situation. It can help us understand the failure of attempts at unique causal analyses of our present situation at the same time that it can provide a basis for helping others to find a ground for rethinking their appropriate roles in the ongoing university activity.

Prospects

☙ 15 ❧

What is the outlook for universities? Internally, neither the political radicals nor the "counterculture" forces of the new consciousness are likely to have more than a limited, although important, effect. Their respective positions go against the nature of the university and so provoke opposition from basic forces. The new consciousness has the effect of acting against the human and social drive to advance knowledge; and political radicalism runs against the claims of intellectual freedom. But, as we have argued, the university has the resilience to recognize neglected values in the demands of both groups, and it has the resources to cope with the many new resultant problems that fall within its mission. Physical disruption is totally intolerable. But the internal pressures for change are part of the normal processes of university activity. Even the contemporary expansion of curricular issues into a debate on the nature of the university is itself still part of the healthy working of that process.

But the effect of the political situation on university activity in the seventies and beyond, presents a different prospect unless we develop the means to cope with the anti-intellectualism that seems to be increasingly easier to trigger. Of course, there always have been anti-intellectual strands in the American makeup, but for the most part they do not go beyond verbal and social expressions of dislike. Also the involvement of federal agencies such as HEW during the sixties was not a reason for concern. Some officials were of course persuaded by the advocates of change that they must act to move the backward universities from their hidebound stance. The indication, however, was that these officials' actions would have amounted to little more than appointing study commissions, bureaus, or agencies. But in the 1970 period, official pressure came from the top leadership in the national government—from the President indirectly, but from the Vice President in an aggressive, persistent attack. He attacked presidents of leading universities and advised that political leftists on the faculty and in the student body of universities be eliminated. Apparently he believed that criminal acts on campus justified his attacks on universities. We agree that criminal acts of violence should clearly be treated as such—that the criminals should be caught, brought to trial with due process, and properly punished if found guilty. But to elevate this normal process to political and legislative action is to reinforce the radicals' belief that all normal police and judicial processes are expressions of a repressive politics. When police use force that is not necessary to their safety, the responses to these actions validate the radicals' beliefs that the police will radicalize more students and underline Senator Chase's warning that repressive actions will follow all such radicalization.

Prospects for the seventies and beyond must be gauged from this perspective. Of course, no dramatic immediate damage to university activity seems likely, and as elections come and go, the anti-intellectual temperature varies. Yet the situation is volatile, and we suspect that the repressive tendency can be quite explosive. We will accordingly consider three possibilities: immediate political counteraction from the universities in response to crises of the sort that marked the Fall of 1970; a basic shift back to comparatively favorable conditions for autonomous university activity; and the long-run view and the line of action this shift suggests.

In this book we have sought to minimize the "politicization" of the universities, but the purpose was, in part, to keep "clean" the lines of political action open to its members. As individuals, they can associate their interests with the university and identify themselves accordingly, so long as this activity is kept distinct from the official acts of the institution. The Princeton plan for the election campaign of 1970 illustrates how these principles may be applied consistently and appropriately in a critical situation.

In a broader view, there is the question of the prospects for restoring and maintaining the climate of opinion in which universities can function freely in conducting fundamental inquiries. The climate will be only speciously favorable if it depends on the belief that academic thought is, or ought to be, insulated from ongoing sociopolitical issues. The views of Professor Roche of Brandeis can be interpreted to encourage this misleading belief, for he reported with emphatic approval the fact that neither he nor Herbert Marcuse used their classrooms to win adherents for their partisan political positions, but instead restricted themselves to teaching political theory. The classroom is not a place for political campaigning, as Professor Roche says, but the alternative to this is not neutral professors and remote subject matters. The criteria for what is admissible in a university classroom are the disciplined rigor of thought in what is presented, and its total openness to sharp attack. When these criteria are satisfied, and when alternative courses are available, an academic course may properly be politically controversial. As Watson should teach and defend his theory of the double helix, so Marcuse should teach *One-Dimensional Man* and attack the system and thus open himself to full counterattack. Sidney Hook's arguments, like Roche's, can have the effect of encouraging leaders whose tendencies are repressive in this respect. (We are not here taking up the actual position of Roche and Hook but only the kind of effect it may have.) Where are the counter-tendencies to come from?

The restoration of the needed climate depends, we believe, on a group whose membership is not to be identified in terms of such lables as "liberal," "conservative," "silent majority," and so on. Rather, members of this group should be drawn from the increasing number of university-trained minds, and from persons in rapport with them, in business, science, politics, communications, and the arts. Boards of trustees of public and private universities are made up of such people for the most part. Similarly, the members of the Presidential Commission on Campus Unrest reflected the diversity of persons who make up this group. They must continually judge the developing situation to determine whether the universities' difficulties—those involving the relations of universities to society—are deepening or, more hopefully, relaxing. The university training of persons in this group enables them to have an authentic awareness of the values to be guarded, the standards to be applied, and the power to make right judgments about such a developing situation. The university must in large measure work through them, recognizing that their interest in and effectiveness on behalf of the university depends on how good a job the institution had done in their student years.

The influence of these persons can be exerted perhaps most significantly on the national leadership; for just as the most dangerous repressive tendencies are those coming from this leadership, so the change in climate needs to be stimulated by it. The Presidential Commission on Campus Unrest in 1970 showed a clear grasp of the problem and pointed the way toward a solution. It sought to formulate a unified national response to university problems and appealed for Presidential leadership in such an effort. A great opportunity was lost when the Vice President interpreted the appeal as an expectation that the President should "replace the campus cop." This interpretation belittled the report, the President, the campus "cop," and the real issues involved. Mr. Agnew purported to hedge his attack by limiting his remarks to criticisms of criminals, but he also swung widely at all social criticism that deviated from his narrow position (he included those of Senators of his own party). The issue, therefore, was not one of pursuing criminals, but of making deviant political or social theory in a university a criminal undertaking.

The prospects of the nation itself are in question when the difficulty appears in this form of an impasse between blue-ribbon citizens on the one hand, who are seeking to secure the university's place in a unified society, and, on the other, the political leadership that treats open intellectual inquiry as a threat to the flag. That the blue-ribbon citizens have the attitude they do is the best reason for hope, but their stand must be made as firm and clear as possible if they are to succeed, for in time of danger intellectual freedom can seem a threat to a needed stability of policy; and fearful political rhetoric sometimes succeeds in unexpected places.

The Voiceless University

Confronted with such rhetoric, it is not enough simply to praise freedom of inquiry or to argue only in general terms that criticism is compatible with loyalty to the "system." The issue is whether the two are compatible in this country at this time. The actual condition of higher education in some other states is so bad that free inquiry in them would be subversive. The confidence shown by the blue-ribbon group in the United States rests on more than the procedures for change provided by the system; it rests also on a belief in the bases of national greatness and the disposition of the nation to cope with new difficulties in a spirit of freedom. Insofar as the group has this attitude it is more "loyal" than Mr. Agnew of 1970. But, for the same reason, it also has a basis of communication with the political leadership, possibly even with Agnew.

Plato sets one of his dialogues in the period after Athens had lost its major war to Sparta and had its empire destroyed. Plato evidently felt that political support for and openness to fundamental inquiries about the public good were sorely needed. He treated these inquiries as compatible with a concrete appreciation of Athens' remarkable political and cultural achievements. Perhaps he believed that Athens could discover new and great leaders and recapture her earlier greatness. In this dialogue, *Meno,* an Athenian politician states the narrow-minded position of the politician who fears intellectual activity and considers it a source of subversion. Anytus supports patriotism, nationalism, and duty, and fears the Sophists, the "university" teachers of the ancient Greek world. He was one of those who later brought Socrates to trial for corrupting the youth and for unorthodox religious beliefs. Athens never regained the cultural and political leadership she had enjoyed.

We are not analogizing the contemporary situation in our country to that of Athens in the post-Peloponnesian War period. But we do see a telltale sign of the state of our society in the relationship of universities to our national leadership. Small changes in the breadth of outlook of national leadership can well have cumulative effects, and the country's prospects are tied to those of the university. The university produces future leaders by educating youths who are sensitive to our best values (including those which enable the country to undergo independent scrutiny) and eager to challenge our basic ills.

However, immediate issues of legislation and elections and the concern for restoring favorable conditions should not cause us to lose sight of the long-range basis for hope. The prospects of the university that are rooted simply in the vitality of intellectual activity are as promising as always. We express this confidence, and enjoy the values bound up with it, when we insist during these times on maintaining the continuity of the classroom course and the autonomy of intellectual activities in the university.

Index

A

Academic freedom: and drug use, 84; intellectual basis of, 177; as issue, 3; and political radicalism, 180

Academic politics, 38

Academy, Greek, 1, 154

ACE Special Committee on Campus Tension, 150

Administration: and cancellation of classes, 14; charges against, 67; and communication gap, 36; and concept of central problem, 33, 35; and drug problem, 86–87; in knowledge-power relation, 44; response to demonstration by, 54; response to 1964–1969 revolt by, 3, 7, 9; student dialogue with, 74; and student judiciary at Stony Brook, 56

AGNEW, S., 181, 183, 184

ANAXAGORAS, 84

Antiauthoritarianism, 150, 153

ARCHIMEDES, 21

ARISTOTLE, 23, 51, 111n, 173

AUGUSTINE, 159

Authoritarianism, 14, 21, 79, 147, 149, 152

Autonomous ideas: abstract vs. concrete, 29; as abstraction from experience, 94, 106–107; adaptations of methods to, 153; as central, 31; continuity of, 103–105; and criteria of completeness, 109, 110; extensions of, 104–105, 121–122; and feeling vs. reasoning, 30; five relations of, 93, 96, 98, 101; in Gibbon, 131; as psychological, 146, 153; as a search for patterns, 127; source of life in, 29, 31; in Trotsky, 132–133; as an unfolding, 115; as a unique instance, 119. *See also* Shared ideas

B

BACON, F., 22

Berkeley, University of California at, 4

BETTELHEIM, B., 157

BOYER, C. B., 92n

C

Change: absence in core activity of, 175; from advance of knowledge, 174; and broad bases of action, 71; curricular, 24; effect on idea of university of, 1; as an end, 166; and developmental and neohumanist theories, 167; history of educational, 173; metaphysical doctrine of, 173; ultimate determinants of, 176

Chicago, University of, 137

City College of New York, 84

Classrooms and classroom activity: arguments against, 15–16, 24;

and "authority complex," 146;
as basis of confidence, 185;
and books, 32; breakdowns in,
14; as center of educational
process, 25, 27; cancellation of,
14; communication in, 20; conception of, 10; cumulative experience in, 87; and curricular
innovation, 23; deemphasis of,
10; definitions of, 17, 25; and
democratic structure, 82; disciplined inquiry in, 17; diversity of, 25; egalitarian approach
to, 150; and free-form discussion, 25; and independent
study, 28; and larger university
life, 35, 40, 43; limits and
weaknesses of, 135, 147; methods in, 147; and model of
dialogue, 150; novelty in, 170;
and participation in governance, 78; psychological and
social effect of, 87–88; situation of, 19; social structure of,
149; strikes against, 14; as
structure of discourse, 23–24;
university level of, 20
Communication: and ACE report,
150; in classroom, 20, 150;
professional gap in, 36–40;
between students and administration, 74; in terms of discipline, 22
Confrontations, 34
Consciousness, New or III, 170–171,
180
Cornell, 6
Creativity, 10, 15, 16, 65, 72. *See
also* Innovation
Curriculum: and action, 71; and
classroom system, 23–24; and
credit for extramural activity,
67; cycles in, 23; as determined by internal standards,
176; distribution requirements
of, 66; relevance of, 69, 70;
student determination of, 8;

student orientation of, 64–73;
specialization in, 64, 66; stimulation of, 71; time-lag in restructuring, 174
Curricular illustration: bases of unity
in, 137; broader problems of,
136; interdisciplinary scope of,
135; linking disciplines in, 137;
objectives of, 145; relations of
courses in, 140

D

DARWIN, C., 166, 173
*Decline and Fall of the Roman Em-
pire, The,* 131–133
DEDEKIND, 101
Demonstrations: administration response to, 54; aims of, 55–57;
evaluation of, 56–57; as a first
step, 52–53; major causes of,
50; potentialities of, 40–41;
warrant for, 40–41;
DESCARTES, 98, 101
Developmental theory of education,
167–170
Disruptions. *See* Demonstrations
Disciplines and disciplined thought,
11, 17, 19, 22–26, 37, 46, 47,
70, 178; in interdisciplinary
program, 138–139; knowledge
of as best hope, 60; ways of
presenting, 20. *See also* Classrooms and classroom activity
Discussion or lecture, 150–151
DOSTOYEVSKY, F., 114
Drugs, 3, 5, 42, 84–88

E

Educational process: center of, 25, 30;
and communications media,
16; concern for whole person
in, 15; developmental theory
of, 167–170; and elitism, 45;
failures in, 78; as holistic patterning, 16; internal determination of, 176; living and
learning in, 8; methods vs.

Index

matter in, 15; neohumanist theory of, 9; psychological approach to, 22; subjective-objective, 22–25; as a "system," 23

Elitism, 45–47

Environmental Defense Fund, 58

Establishment, 6, 7, 9, 33, 52, 54, 168

EUCLID, 89, 92, 97–98, 103, 104

EUDOXUS, 101

EVES, H., 103n

F

Faculty. *See* Classrooms and classroom activity, Piecemeal approach, Teachers and teaching, University

G

GAVORSE, J., 125n

GENOVESE, E., 170

GIBBON, E., 131–133

Globular approach: to campus problems, 42; and drug use, 84; to ideas, 169

Governance, 4, 5, 6, 33–34, 55–56, 74–82

Grades, 9, 153–155; and student dignity, 155

H

HARRISON, R., 148n

Harvard University, 137

HATFIELD, M., 3n

HAYAKAWA, S., 9

Hazen Foundation, 167

HEMINGWAY, E., 123

HERODOTUS, 124–131

Higher education, theory of: and classroom system, 24; distorted problems of, 63; overemphasis on change in, 173; and power analysis, 34; psychological approach to, 10, 11; shifts in fashion in, 171; sociopolitical approach to, 10; starting point of, 11

HOBBES, T., 104

HOOK, S., 182

Hughes Committee, 5n

HUME, D., 125

I

Idealism, 50–61; and action, 52, 54, 57, 58–61; in revolutionary approach, 52–53; and youth, 50–51

Identity of individual, 15, 24, 79, 88; and classroom activity, 25–27; in developmental theory, 167; and religion, 156. *See also* Individuals

Independent study, 23, 28, 67, 77, 147

Individuals, 15, 16, 25–27, 31, 64, 71, 88, 167; vs. Establishment, 168; life organization of, 159; need of holistic perspective by, 156–157; security of, 157–160. *See also* Identity

Innovation: and classroom system, 23; continuity in, 103; and course presentation, 20; evidence of need for, 153; and internalized learning, 147; vs. routine in educational method, 15–16

Intelligence, enraged, 58

J

JAMES, W., 158

JOYCE, J., 172

K

KAHLER, E., 172

KANT, E., 78, 160, 162

King Lear, 108–120

KUHN, T. S., 24

L

LANGER, S., 171

LASCH, C., 170

Law enforcement and student unrest, 34

189

Index

Learners, power of, 60

Learning: as auditory experience, 15; developmentalist view of, 168; discovery in, 149, 153; experience and action in, 69; and genuineness, 65; internal vs. external sources of, 147; and living, 8; plan-as-you-go, 14; from predisciplinary to disciplinary, 169; professional, 168; as reinvention, 149; self-directed, 147, 154; subjective-objective, 22–24. *See also* Teachers and teaching, Teacher-learning relation

LINCOLN, A., 68

LINNAEUS, 166

Lyceum, 1, 154

LYSENKO, 175

M

MAC LEAN, N., 111n, 118n

MARCUSE, H., 53, 156, 182

MARX, K., 53, 156

Meno, 184

MILTON, J., 32, 153

Mind-matter opposition, 23–25

Moderates and radicalism, 4–6, 10

MUELLER, H. J., 122

Multiversity, 2

Myth, interest in, 157–158, 162

N

NADER, R., 42

Neohumanism, 167–170

Neo-Marxist analysis of university problems, 34–35

New York Times, 6n, 150n

NEWMAN, J. H., 1

NEWSON, C. V., 103n

NEWTON, I., 30, 102, 161

NIXON, R. M., 4, 181

Novelty: and dependence on structure in art, 171–172; in transmission of values, 170

O

Open admissions, 35, 46

ORTEGA Y GASSET, 47

P

PAULING, L., 38

PERICLES, 84

Philosophy in a New Key, 171

Philosophy of higher education. *See* Higher education, University

Piecemeal approach: to campus problems, 41–43; in development of ideas, 31; to change, 171; vs. globular method, 42

PINTER, H., 172

PLATO, 22, 46, 82, 169, 173; the *Meno* of, 46, 184; the *Republic* of, 19n, 122, 151, 155, 156; teaching approach in works of, 151

POINCARE, H., 149

Police, 3, 4, 41, 52, 84–87, 181

Political pressures on the university, 181–183

Power analysis: and basis of dialogue, 77; focus on constituencies in, 36; in governance, 75; of main university problem, 33–34; and organization of university, 44

Presidential Commission on Campus Unrest, 182–183

Princeton plan, 181

Professional activity, 14, 21; and communication gap, 46–50; and organization of university, 45

Psychological approach: explanations of unrest through, 34; recent values of, 146–147; in "super-organism" of *Walden II,* 46; to university's failure, 10; as way of presenting discipline, 20

PYTHAGORAS, 46, 93, 97–102, 106

190

Index

Index

raged intelligence, 58; and idealism, 58; as not communicated, 36

University classroom, uniqueness of, 20

University community: of communities, 45, 48; elitist view of, 45–47; life of, 38–40; model of diversity, 39; and shared ideas, 41, 47; and social action programs, 50, 181; spontaneist view of, 47–49

Uses of the Past, 122

W

WALD, G., 51

WATSON, J., 30, 38, 68, 182

WHITEHEAD, A. N., 60–61, 94n, 160–161, 169, 175, 177

WILDER, R. L., 103n